Bioengineering

Discover How Nature Inspires Human Designs

WITH 25 PROJECTS

Christine
Burillo-Kirch, PhD

ILLUSTRATED BY ALEXIS CORNELL

~ Latest science titles in the *Build It Yourself* Series ~

Check out more titles at www.nomadpress.net

Nomad Press
A division of Nomad Communications
10 9 8 7 6 5 4 3 2 1

This book was manufactured by Marquis Book Printing,
Montmagny, Québec, Canada
August 2016, Job #125558

ISBN Softcover: 978-1-61930-370-6
ISBN Hardcover: 978-1-61930-366-9

Educational Consultant, Marla Conn

Questions regarding the ordering of this book should be addressed to
Nomad Press
2456 Christian St.
White River Junction, VT 05001
www.nomadpress.net

Printed in Canada.

(PS) Interested in Primary Sources?

Look for this icon. Use a smartphone or tablet app to scan the QR code and explore more about bioengineering! You can find a list of URLs on the Resources page.

If the QR code doesn't work, try searching the Internet with the Keyword Prompts to find other helpful sources.

bioengineering 🔎

3000 BCE: Imhotep, an Egyptian architect, engineer, and physician, practices medicine. He is so revered that people consider him a god.

1000 BCE: The first known "hospital" is built in Greece.

1505: Leonardo da Vinci draws a flight machine called an ornithopter, based on the mechanics of bird and bat wings. He also draws many accurate pictures of human anatomy.

1546: Girolamo Fracastoro, an Italian physician, discusses contagions, which are microbes that cause disease.

1606: Galileo Galilei, a famous Italian astronomer and scientist, builds a thermoscope, studies skeletal load, and influences the medical field to take patients' heart rates.

1961: Marshall Nirenberg, Johann Matthaei, and Maxine Singer determine the codes in RNA required to make each amino acid found within a protein.

1963: Otto Schmitt coins the term "biomimetics."

1977: American scientists Allan Maxam and Walter Gilbert develop DNA sequencing, which allows scientists to read the DNA code of different genes.

1810: Nicolas Appert introduces the method of canning to preserve food.

1953: Using Rosalind Franklin's work as a model, James Watson and Francis Crick determine the structure of DNA.

2012: Several teams of scientists develop and refine a technology called CRISPR/Cas9, which allows scientists to change any gene.

1983–87: Kary Mullis develops polymerase chain reaction (PCR), a technique that makes multiple copies of a particular gene. After PCR, this gene product can be used in DNA sequencing, followed by introduction into a new organism.

TIMELINE

1954: The first organ transplant occurs. A kidney is donated from one identical twin to the other (humans have two and need only one to survive).

1950: Richard Feynman first discusses the concept of nanotechnology.

1933: Thomas Hunt Morgan, an American scientist, earns the Nobel Prize in Medicine for his work showing that genes are the units of heredity.

2003: The Human Genome Project, an international effort to determine the code of the entire set of human genes, is completed.

1997: German botanists Wilhelm Barthlott and Christoph Neinhuis look at the chemical composition and structure behind the self-cleaning ability of the lotus flower. Scientists develop nanotechnology that mimics the self-cleaning effect for items from cars to clothes.

1928: Alexander Fleming, an American scientist, discovers penicillin, the first antibiotic.

1990: The first bioengineered strain of yeast is produced.

1996: Dolly the sheep is born; she is the first cloned mammal.

1895: Wilhelm Conrad Röntgen, a German physicist, discovers X-rays.

1885: French scientist and inventor Count Hilaire Bernigaud de Chardonnet creates "artificial silk," which results in the textile rayon.

1831: Michael Faraday invents the generator.

1866: "The Father of Genetics," an Austrian monk named Gregor Mendel, publishes his historic breeding experiments in pea plants.

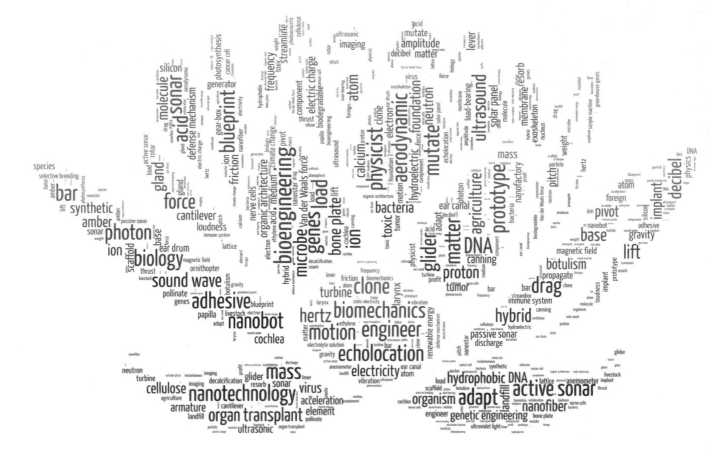

WHAT IS

Have you ever looked at a bird and wished that you could fly? Do you want to swim as gracefully as a dolphin in the ocean? You are not alone!

For thousands of years, people have looked to nature for ideas to solve problems. Nature has provided us with the inspiration needed to create tools and make devices, such as airplanes to take us to new heights. **Engineers** use the principles of **physics** to invent, design, and build things, such as devices, machines, and tools.

Bioengineering

engineer: someone who uses science, math, and creativity to design products or processes to meet human needs or solve problems.

physics: the science of how matter and energy work together. Matter is what an object is made of. Energy is the ability to perform work.

biology: the study of living things.

bioengineering: the use of engineering principles applied to biological function to build devices, tools, or machines for a human need.

organism: any living thing, such as a plant or animal.

genes: inherited material that has the instructions to make an organism with certain traits and characteristics.

microbe: an organism that is so small it can be seen only with a microscope.

adapt: to change in response to something.

species: a group of living things that are closely related and can produce young.

WORDS TO KNOW

Biology is the study of life and living things. **Bioengineering** is a combination of biology and engineering. Bioengineering is the process of applying engineering principles to biological functions to fulfill human needs.

The word *bioengineering* is a general term that describes several areas of study. These include biomedical engineering, biological engineering, and biomimetics, which we will discuss later in the book. Each of these areas focuses on specific needs, such as medicine or energy, but there is also a lot of overlap between these areas.

We'll look at these three different types of bioengineering in this book. For example, biomedical engineers try to solve medical problems by making unique devices that are specific to certain medical needs.

Have you ever seen someone with an artificial limb? In this case, biology provides a model, or a real limb, for engineers to think about while they design and create an artificial limb. The artificial limb works almost as well as the missing limb would have worked.

Some biological engineers study how an **organism** might be changed to solve certain problems. One problem biological engineers try to solve is how to grow certain plants in different climates.

Organisms are made of cells, and each cell contains **genes**. The genes provide the instructions inside a cell that determine what an organism is going to be. The genes in a tomato will only contain instructions to make a tomato, never a squash. Biological engineers search for ways of altering genes to improve the organism. For example, a tomato plant can be altered so that it can grow with less water. This allows the tomato plant to be grown in areas that get less rain.

Did You Know?

The Human Genome Project began more than 25 years ago. In 2003, scientists provided a map and code of all the human genes in our genome!

Biomimetics combines the functionality of nature, or how something in nature works, with human needs.

Trees, plants, **microbes**, and some animal life have existed on the earth for far longer than humans. These living things have had to **adapt** during millions of years to remain alive as a **species**. People who study biomimetics believe that nature comes up with the best possible solutions to different situations and problems. During the course of millions of years, many difficulties have arisen that nature has had to overcome!

Studying how something works in nature can give us ideas on how to do things better ourselves. Scientists can mimic the process they discover in nature to fulfill a human need. Some of the items or devices we use every day were designed with the help of nature. Biomimetics looks to nature to get ideas for using electricity, sound waves, adhesives, and lots of other materials and processes.

Velcro was partially developed based on the design of the burdock plant. The inventor was inspired by the way the plant's burrs attached to his clothes and his dog's fur.

We use energy every day to light our homes, power our cars, and charge our laptops. Scientists and engineers have been working to harness the power in nature into a force we can control. Wind, water, and sun are all forms of renewable energy that are better for the planet than coal and oil. We might be able to come up with ways to have enough energy while keeping the earth and ourselves healthier.

Here are more problems that bioengineering has solved.

Problem	Solution	How
Noise pollution made by trains going through tunnels	Change train nose into a cone shape that resembles a kingfisher bird beak	Train nose allows air to flow more easily around it
Heart arrhythmia	Pacemaker	Electrical signal keeps the heartbeat regular
Long wait for transplant organs	Artificial heart	Can replace a human heart for a period of one to two years

This book looks at several different areas of science and engineering that use bioengineering to create and improve products and processes. These include agriculture, energy, medicine, and items in our household. Just about every field benefits from the observation of how the natural world works!

Some Bioengineering History

While the term *bioengineering* was first used in the 1950s, people have been practicing bioengineering for much, much longer. When you are trying to solve a problem, it's natural to look to the environment around you for answers. It is also fun to observe nature do its thing every day.

The next time you are outside, take a moment to look at something going on in nature. Perhaps you'll stumble upon an ant colony moving food or look closely at the bark on different trees. What can you learn from your observations?

One of the first people to document their use of bioengineering was Leonardo da Vinci. He was an Italian artist, scientist, and thinker who lived from 1452 to 1519. Da Vinci was interested in just about everything, from science, mathematics, and medicine to architecture and aviation. He drew lots of pictures and wrote down his ideas in a set of notebooks.

PS

Flight of Birds

Da Vinci kept careful records of his observations in his notebooks. You can see da Vinci's diagrams and read his thoughts on birds and flight in a document called *Codex on the Flight of Birds*. Do you recognize any scientific principles as ones you've studied before?

da Vinci Codex Flight Birds

Da Vinci looked at birds flying when he was thinking about how to design a flying machine. By 1505, Leonardo da Vinci had drawn many illustrations related to flight based on his observations. He marveled at the wings of birds, studied their skeletal structure, and observed their flight **motion** and patterns in the presence and absence of wind.

Da Vinci and other researchers learned the basic principles of physics by watching the world around him.

- Da Vinci's use of nature to model a flight machine is the essence of biomimetics. His flight machine, the **ornithopter**, was based on his observations of birds and bats. We still study birds in flight to find ways to improve the transportation industry!

- Galileo Galilei was a brilliant Italian astronomer, **physicist**, mathematician, and engineer who lived in the 1600s. He looked at how the skeletal structures of particular animals could support their **weights**. Galileo was fascinated by the structure, design, and strength of bones in regard to how much **load**, or weight, the bones could carry.

He realized that larger animals needed thicker bones to carry the heavier weight. There was a limit to how large an animal could be. This is called the scaling law and it has uses in many different fields, including medicine and structural engineering.

• Farmers have always looked to nature to improve their harvests. Bountiful crops are affected by many different factors, including sun, water, soil, and pests. More recently, they've added genetics to that list. Genetics is the science of understanding DNA, genes, and inheritance. Genes are small units that contain DNA, the information and instructions that make livings things the way they are. Scientists have altered the DNA of certain crops to increase the chances that a harvest will be productive.

• Modern medicine is another area that has benefited greatly from advances in bioengineering. In the 1960s, John Charnley developed an artificial hip joint after studying how real hip joints worked. He developed an **implant** that was similar in structure and moved well. Today, scientists are working on many different types of artificial joints and limbs to help people. They are also discovering new ways of delivering medicine and helping the body to fight disease using bioengineering.

Bioengineering

The world of bioengineering is as large as our collective imaginations can make it. It involves many different fields of science, and the fun part is figuring out how they are all connected!

Each chapter of this book begins with an essential question to help guide your exploration of bioengineering. Keep the question in your mind as you read the chapter. At the end of each chapter, use your bioengineering notebook to record your thoughts and answers.

? ESSENTIAL QUESTION

What product do you use in your own house that was created through bioengineering?

Engineering Design Process

Every bioengineer keeps a notebook with the details of the engineering design process. Bioengineers use a design method that is very similar to the method that engineers use. As you read through this book and do the activities, keep track of your observations, data, and designs in an engineering design worksheet, like the one shown here. When doing an activity, remember that there is no right answer or right way to approach a project. Be creative and have fun!

Problem: What problem are we trying to solve?

Research: Has anything been invented to help solve the problem? What can we learn?

Question: Are there any special requirements for the device? An example of this is a car that must go a certain distance in a certain amount of time.

Brainstorm: Draw lots of designs for your device and list the materials you are using!

Prototype: Build the design you drew during brainstorming.

Test: Test your **prototype** and record your observations.

Evaluate: Analyze your test results. Do you need to make adjustments? Do you need to try a different prototype?

Think About Backyard Bioengineering

Bioengineering has been around for a long time. People look to nature to design products that fit certain needs. We can also simply observe nature and see how it works.

For example, cats are very good at keeping themselves clean and removing loose cat fur. Have you ever touched a cat's tongue? What do you notice about it? How can you use your observations to improve a product that many of us already use every day?

1 Spend some time observing nature at different times during the day. Look at the sky, plants, animals, and insects. What else do you notice? Do you see a cobweb or bird's nest? Why is it useful to observe things at different times of the day?

2 Create a chart in your science journal like the one below. Fill it with your observations and how they might be useful.

What I observed nature doing	Describe what nature used	Possible human need	Possible product
cat licking fur	rough tongue	untangle hair	hairbush

THINK MORE: What do other animals do to clean their fur? How are their methods different from a cat's? How are they similar? Design a prototype based on the hygiene habits of a different animal. How does it work? What would you design differently?

Chapter 1

BIOENGINEERING IN COMMUNICATION AND SOUND WAVES

Have you ever thought about communication and how much we need it? We communicate every day with our family, friends, and teachers—we talk, we listen, and many of us take it for granted.

Not all communication results in sounds that we can hear. Some communication is nonverbal, including reading something that is written, hand movements, gestures, and sign language. But when you listen to your teacher explain a lesson or when you talk to your friend about a movie, you are using **sound waves** to communicate.

ESSENTIAL QUESTION

What are the different ways that sound is used in bioengineering?

Bioengineers use what we know about sound waves to develop instruments that transform sound waves into images that we can see. Sound waves are also important when designing hearing aid devices.

Sound Waves

Sound is just a **vibration**. It is a movement from an object or substance that makes the surrounding gas, liquid, or solid **particles** move in waves.

Put your hand on your throat over your voice box, or **larynx**. Sing a song or say something silly—do you feel the vibration? When air moves through your larynx, it vibrates and produces a sound wave. This wave continues to move through the air or water or even solid **matter**, such as a door! It can move through anything that has **molecules**. Sound can actually travel through water more quickly than through air. A sound wave, or vibration of molecules, cannot occur in an area that has no molecules.

The sound wave can move quickly or slowly, depending on the medium it is traveling in.

WORDS TO KNOW

sound wave: the invisible vibrations in the air that you hear as sound.

vibration: a quick back-and-forth movement.

particle: a tiny piece of matter.

larynx: the organ that produces sound in the human body, also known as a voice box.

matter: anything that takes up space and has mass.

molecule: a very small particle made of combinations of atoms.

medium: any gas, liquid, or solid material containing matter.

Have you ever dropped a pebble in a lake? Just as the water ripples outward from the pebble in waves, sound waves travel in all directions away from the object making the sound. The sound waves lose energy over time and become weaker until they stop completely.

When we hear sound from an instrument, what is happening? Every instrument has a vibrating **component**. String instruments, such as pianos, violas, cellos, banjos, violins, and guitars, have vibrating strings that produce sounds.

Other instruments have different vibrating parts. A drum has a vibrating **membrane**. A xylophone has vibrating steel bars. What about a flute? A flute is a wooden or metal tube with holes—what could be vibrating?

A flute is a wind instrument. All wind instruments already have air inside. When a musician blows into a flute, the air column inside the flute is disturbed by the additional air. The air column itself vibrates, and as the sound waves travel back and forth, they create sound.

Try This!

You can see sound vibrations with a rubber band! Cut open a rubber band so it is one long, stretchy piece. Attach one end to a stationary object and the other end to a different stationary object, such as the two sides of a shoe box. Now, pluck the rubber band. Do you hear sound? Do you see the vibration? The vibration of the rubber band is what produces the sound.

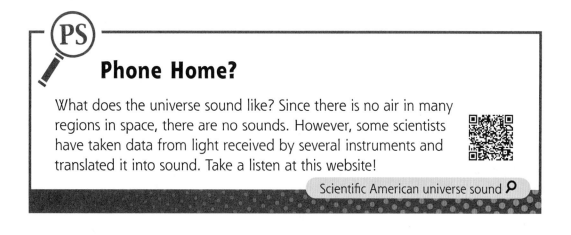

(PS)

Phone Home?

What does the universe sound like? Since there is no air in many regions in space, there are no sounds. However, some scientists have taken data from light received by several instruments and translated it into sound. Take a listen at this website!

Scientific American universe sound 🔍

Sound has different characteristics, including **loudness** and **pitch**. Loudness is determined by the height, or **amplitude**, of the sound waves. Pitch, or the high or low tone, is determined by the **frequency** of the sound waves.

The taller the sound wave, the louder the sound. The greater the number of sound waves that occur within a set amount of time, the higher the tone or pitch. What would a sound

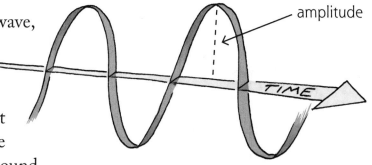

wave look like if you were whispering in a low tone of voice to a friend? What would a sound wave look like if you were yelling at the top of your lungs in a high tone of voice? Try drawing what these different waves look like.

Pitch is measured in **hertz**. A high-sounding voice has a high frequency, or a high number of waves per second. The loudness of a sound is measured in **decibels**, which is abbreviated as dB. A loud voice has a high decibel number. Can you draw a sound wave with a high hertz and high decibel? Would the sound be a loud, high tone sound or a loud, low tone sound?

Humans can hear a specific range of frequencies and decibels. Our ears can hear sounds with a pitch between 20 and 20,000 hertz and loudness between 0 dB and 80 dB. Somewhere between 110 and 120 dB, sound becomes painful for the human ear.

We can only hear sounds that reach our ears. The sound waves enter our **ear canal** and cause the membrane of the **ear drum** to vibrate. The vibration is then transmitted to three small bones within the middle ear.

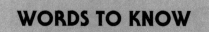

Much like in a game of dominos, the vibration gets passed along within the ear.

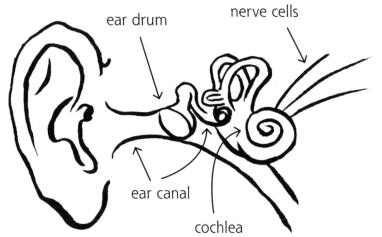

Eventually, it reaches the **cochlea** of the inner ear. Here, different areas recognize different frequencies, or pitches. Certain **nerve cells** send this information up to the brain. Since this happens at lightning speed, the sound feels **instantaneous**.

Do you or anyone you know have hearing aids? Bioengineers developed hearing aids to help people who have trouble hearing. In the past, people who had trouble hearing used ear trumpets to amplify the sound waves that arrived at their ears.

Once Alexander Graham Bell invented the telephone in the 1870s and people understood how technology could be used to amplify sound, electronic hearing aids were invented. At first these were bulky contraptions that were too large to carry around.

As the technology improved, hearing aids became easy to transport. Soon they were small enough that people could wear them. With the invention of digital computers, hearing aids shrank even more, and now they can fit entirely in the ear canal. You might not even know if someone you're talking to is wearing a hearing aid!

Did You Know?

There are some sounds that we cannot hear. Dogs, cats, and other animals can hear **ultrasonic** frequencies greater than 20,000 hertz. Dolphins and bats can hear frequencies up to 160,000 hertz!

Sonar

Several mammals, such as bats, whales, and dolphins, use sound waves for things other than hearing. They make noises with ultrasonic frequencies that can be used to locate food and communicate with other mammals to gather information regarding the environment.

Which Is Faster, Light or Sound?

The race between light and sound is really no competition. Even though light and sound both travel in waves, light moves almost 1,000,000 times faster than sound! Observe the next thunderstorm in your area. Unless the storm is very close to your house, you will always see the lightning before hearing the thunder!

Using **echolocation**, these animals send out a sound signal that bounces off something in the environment. It returns to the animal with information about where the object is located. The echoing sound waves also relay information such as the size, shape, and type of object.

Bats are especially adept at using echolocation. They use **sonar** to echolocate the fruit and insects they eat, sources of water, their general surroundings, and other bats.

While individual humans usually aren't able to use echolocation to find things with their eyes closed, we have developed a type of echolocation to help us explore places that are hard to get to. Sonar, an acronym for **SO**und **N**avigation **A**nd **R**anging, is the ability to map the location of things in water or air based on the use of sound waves. You might have heard the term "sonar" if you have watched a show or movie involving a submarine.

Submarines and other sea vessels use either passive sonar or active sonar. Passive sonar involves simply listening to noises in the ocean. Active sonar requires sending a sound signal into the water and listening for its echo.

Did You Know?

Walking sticks that use sonar have been developed to help blind people move around more easily.

Holy Jammed Echolocation Signal, Batman!

A recent study found that bats can send a jamming signal to interfere with the echolocation of another bat. Why would they do this? To steal a meal that another bat has found! A species of moth called a tiger moth can also jam a bat's signal and avoid being eaten by the predator bat. The tiger moth makes ultrasonic clicking noises that confuse the echo signal and make it difficult for the bat to find the moth.

It is amazing what sonar data can reveal about the ocean and its inhabitants. Schools of fish, other sea vessels, and a map of the sea floor can be determined by analyzing data retrieved from the use of sonar. Even submarines, which operate in a stealthy manner by hiding under water from the line of sight, cannot always hide from sonar signals.

Sound is a very important component of several instruments used by doctors, nurses, and technicians. Some medical **imaging** techniques use sound waves to capture images of the inside of a body. For example, **ultrasound** scans allow a doctor to see an unborn baby within a pregnant woman's uterus.

Bioengineering

Ultrasound equipment uses sonar! Just as bats and dolphins use active sonar to locate an object, ultrasound scans use high-frequency sound waves to locate an organ or baby, which bounces the sound waves back to the equipment. The computer processes the sound waves into an image that we can see.

While images such as these provide a lot of information, the results are often blurry the deeper you get into the body. Biomedical engineers are currently working on fine-tuning a technique called **photoacoustic** imaging that utilizes both light and sound to produce crisper images.

This technique can already detect individual cancer cells in blood.

Maybe the technique will give doctors and scientists the ability to look at individual brain cells in the future.

Did You Know?

Dolphins use sonar to find their food, since their eyesight isn't very good. They can even find food that is buried under the surface of the sand! Learn more in this video about dolphin sonar.

Animal Planet dolphin sonar 🔍

Communicating Without Sound

There are more ways to communicate than with just sound. Have you ever been unable to talk or been in a country when you were unable to speak the language? If you want to communicate with someone in these instances, what do you do? Use hand signals? Point? Make different facial expressions?

People who don't have the ability to hear can communicate using sign language with others who understand sign language. But for most people, communicating by using only physical movements can be difficult.

Bees can convey a whole lot of information in one little dance! They perform a waggle dance to other members of the beehive to inform them of a new source of food. The direction in which they waggle, or shake, is the exact direction the other bees need to travel to find the food source. The number of waggle dances they perform indicates the distance. Sounds like a fun, but exhausting, way to convey information!

The population of honey bees around the world is declining. Bioengineers are working to develop robotic honey bees to ensure that people will be able to **pollinate** food crops even if the population of living honey bees shrinks beyond repair. The goal is for these robotic bees to work together without needing instructions from human controllers. An electronic waggle dance is one way the robotic bees might be able to communicate with each other.

? **ESSENTIAL QUESTION**

Now it's time to consider and discuss the Essential Question: What are the different ways that sound is used in bioengineering?

19

Make a Cuica!

paper or plastic cup, or tin can • long piece of yarn or string • paper clip • engineering journal

You can make a loud noise using just a cup, string, and some water. A cuica is a small Brazilian friction drum that produces a loud noise. Let's make a cuica and see how the sound is produced!

1 Have you ever seen another person play a cuica? What did their cuica look like? Try making an instrument like the one in the picture. Can you get it to play music?

2 Draw some more designs in your engineering notebook. How else can you use your cup and string together to produce sounds? Make different prototypes and see which one sounds the best.

3 Try using different materials to design musical instruments. Do these produce different pitches? Record the materials you try and the sounds they make in your engineering notebook. Can you make any conclusions about the materials?

THINK MORE: How is the sound being produced? Think about how the sound waves are traveling. What purpose does the cup serve?

Bee a Nectar Detector!

There are several food sources available to bees in the garden. However, bees have one source in mind when they do their waggle dance. Remember, a bee waggles in the direction of a specific food source, and the number of completed dances indicates the distance to travel. In this activity, one complete dance equals one square in the grid.

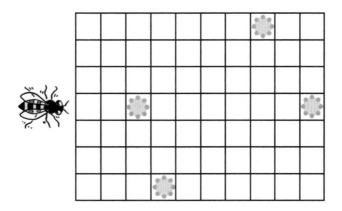

Question #1. This bee waggles in the direction shown and completes the dance three times. Which food source has it found?

Question #2. This bee waggles in the direction shown and completes the dance 10 times. Which food source has it found?

Question #3. This bee waggles in the direction shown and completes the dance eight times. Which food source has it found?

Question #4. This bee waggles in the direction shown and completes the dance four times. Which food source has it found?

THINK MORE: Hide a treasure, then design your own waggle dance to give directions to your friends. Can they find it?

Terrific Tonoscopes

IDEAS FOR SUPPLIES
round container with lid • plastic wrap • salt • PVC pipe connector and PVC pipe joint • engineering journal

A Swiss scientist named Dr. Hans Jenny was very interested in visualizing sound waves. He made a tonoscope to be able to visualize different sound waves made by the mouth. Try making the tonoscope in the picture, and then figure out a design of your own!

1 Cut a hole on one side of the container near the bottom. It should be the same size as the PVC pipe. Cut an inside circle out of the lid so that you are left with an outer plastic ring that can still seal the container.

2 Place the PVC connector on the inside of the container and screw the joint into the connector from the outside, through the hole in the side. This is where you will make a sound that will enter the tonoscope.

3 Cut a piece of plastic wrap large enough to cover the top opening of the container. Place the piece of plastic wrap on the top and make sure it is firmly stretched across the opening. Place the remaining outer portion of the lid over the plastic wrap and seal the container. Tape the free edges of the plastic wrap to the outer portion of the container to ensure a tight membrane at the top.

4 Add 5 tablespoons of salt on top of the plastic membrane. If you are using a smaller-sized container, use less salt. You are now ready to try out the tonoscope!

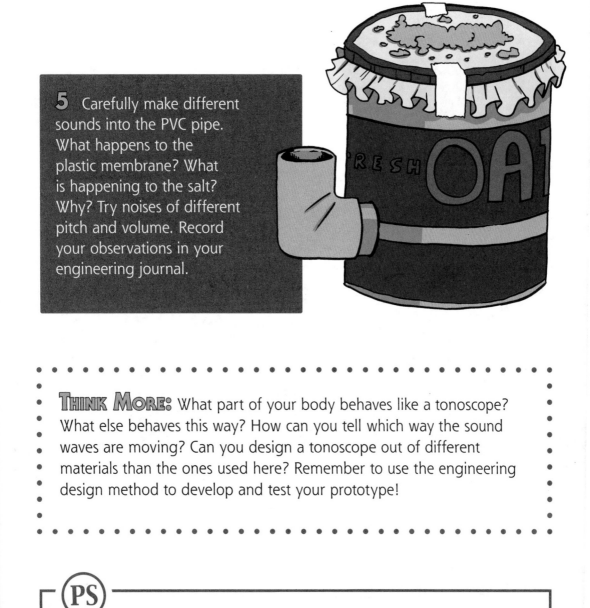

5 Carefully make different sounds into the PVC pipe. What happens to the plastic membrane? What is happening to the salt? Why? Try noises of different pitch and volume. Record your observations in your engineering journal.

THINK MORE: What part of your body behaves like a tonoscope? What else behaves this way? How can you tell which way the sound waves are moving? Can you design a tonoscope out of different materials than the ones used here? Remember to use the engineering design method to develop and test your prototype!

(PS) What Do Voices Look Like?

Human voices make some interesting patterns with a tonoscope! You can see Jenny's assistant working with a tonoscope here.

human voice tonoscope 🔍

What would you do without the heat and light that **electricity** makes possible? Where does electricity come from? In 2014, about 66 percent of the electricity used in the United States came from burning fossil fuels such as coal, oil, and natural gas. Once these fossil fuels are removed from the ground, they cannot be replaced.

Burning non-renewable fossil fuels is damaging to our environment. The process adds **greenhouse gases**, such as carbon dioxide, to our atmosphere. This contributes to **climate change**.

?

ESSENTIAL QUESTION

How does bioengineering help us get the electrical energy we need?

Luckily, there are alternatives to fossil fuels! Bioengineers are working to make **renewable energy** sources more efficient and environmentally friendly. Renewable energy sources include solar energy from the sun, wind power, and **hydroelectric** energy from flowing water. These sources won't run out and are cleaner and often less damaging to our environment.

Did You Know?

Water was first harnessed to do mechanical work more than 2,000 years ago in Greece. Water wheels, or water mills, were used to grind grain into flour.

Renewable energy sources are becoming a more and more popular choice for powering the world.

As they become more common and popular, energy farms that produce and distribute energy are necessary. Before we can talk about renewable energy farms of **solar panels** or wind **turbines**, we need to learn about electricity.

electricity: a form of energy caused by the movement of tiny particles called electrons. It provides power for lights, appliances, video games, and many other electric devices.

greenhouse gases: a gas such as water vapor, carbon dioxide, and methane that traps heat in the atmosphere and contributes to warming temperatures.

climate change: changes to the average weather patterns in an area during a long period of time.

renewable energy: a form of energy that doesn't get used up, including the energy of the sun and the wind.

hydroelectric: generating electricity from the energy of flowing water.

solar panel: a device used to capture sunlight and convert it to usable energy.

turbine: a machine with blades turned by the force of water, air, or steam that changes one type of energy into another.

WORDS TO KNOW

electric charge: when there is an imbalance of electrons, either too many or not enough, and the electrons flow to fix the imbalance.

atom: the smallest particle of matter that cannot be broken down by chemical means. An atom is made up of a nucleus of protons and neutrons, surrounded by a cloud of electrons.

electron: a part of an atom that has a negative charge. It can move from one atom to another.

neutron: a tiny particle inside the center of an atom that carries no charge.

proton: a tiny particle inside the center of an atom that carries a positive charge.

ion: an atom with a positive or negative electrical charge. This means it is missing an electron or has an extra electron.

amber: fossilized tree resin used in early static electricity experiments.

What Is Electricity?

Electricity is the movement of **electric charge** through a wire, which provides power to things that need electrical energy to function. Electrical charge can be found in matter everywhere!

Everything is made of matter—the chair you are sitting on, the house you are living in, and the food you are eating. You are made of matter. All matter is composed of different arrangements of **atoms**, which are the basic building blocks of matter. For example, one type of atom is gold. A piece of pure gold has millions of gold atoms in it and not much else.

Humans, on the other hand, are made up of many different types of atoms and combinations of atoms.

An atom has several parts, including **electrons**, **neutrons**, and **protons**. Electrons are particles that have a negative charge. Protons are particles that have a positive charge. Neutrons are particles that have no charge.

An atom will often have no overall negative or positive charge, due to having the same number of electrons and protons. This keeps the charge balanced.

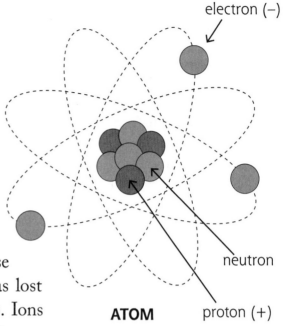

electron (−)

neutron

ATOM

proton (+)

However, the particles of an atom are constantly moving, which means that a portion of the atom could have a quick moment of positive or negative charge. It depends on where the electrons and protons are located at a certain moment in time.

Sometimes, interactions with the environment can cause an atom to lose or gain an electron. An atom that has lost or gained an electron is called an **ion**. Ions can be positive or negative, depending on whether the atom has lost or gained an electron. What happens when an atom gains an electron? Does it have a more slightly negative or positive charge? What happens when an atom loses an electron? Is it slightly more negative or positive?

Did You Know?

The word *electricity* comes from the Latin word *electricus,* which means "like amber."

That's Electric!

An electric charge is caused by the movement of electrons from an area of negative charge toward an area of positive charge. Why are the electrons moving toward an area of positive charge?

A good way to think about electrical charge is to think about magnets. What happens when you put two positively charged magnets together, or two positive poles? Do they attract each other or push each other away? How about a negatively charged magnet and a positively charged magnet? Are they attracted to each other or do they push each other away?

Like charges repel each other, and opposite charges attract each other. This is how electricity works! Electrons are negatively charged and they repel each other. This movement of electrons produces an electrical current.

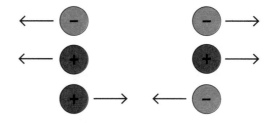

Electricity is not something humans invented. It's something people discovered, and then invented ways of harnessing to make it useful. Around 600 **BCE**, an ancient Greek mathematician named Thales of Miletus performed experiments with a rod of amber and cat fur. He noticed that after the amber rod was rubbed on the cat fur, it gained the ability to attract different things to it, such as a feather. He was seeing **static electricity** in action!

Static electricity is the temporary change in the overall charge (negative or positive) of matter. When you rub two pieces of matter together, such as a balloon and your head, the electrons in those objects are moved around. One object, the balloon, can gain electrons and become temporarily negatively charged on its surface. Other positively charged things, such as your hair or the wall, will now stick to the balloon. Try it!

Remember, negatives and positives attract!

The balloon will eventually return to a neutral state once its charge has been **discharged**. This is what Thales of Miletus discovered with the amber and cat fur.

More than 2,000 years later, Benjamin Franklin performed experiments to demonstrate principles of static electricity, or as he called it, "electrical fire." Many people had thought that electricity and lightning were the same. They both produce light and a cracking sound, have a particular smell, and are attracted to metal.

Franklin's kite-flying experiment was one of several experiments to show that lightning is electricity. According to legend, he flew a kite in a lightning storm with a key attached to the end of the string. When the key gave him an electric shock, he knew that the lightning from the storm was the same thing as electricity.

Historians doubt that this experiment actually happened. It is a very dangerous thing to do! Franklin's major contribution was the development of the lightning rod, which provides safety for homes during lightning storms. A lightning rod attracts the electricity and sends it through a cable into the ground without damaging the building.

(PS) In the Mail

Benjamin Franklin wrote many letters about his experiments with electricity. You can read some of them at this website. Do you think Franklin followed the scientific method? Why or why not?

Franklin experiments archive 🔍

WORDS TO KNOW

armature: the spinning part of a motor, made of tightly coiled wires.

magnetic field: the invisible area around a magnet that pulls objects to it or pushes them away.

generator: a machine that converts mechanical energy into electricity.

anemometer: a device that measures wind speed and pressure.

rotor: the rotating part of a generator.

gearbox: a unit within a machine with interlocking toothed wheels.

Generating a Generator

In 1831, an English scientist named Michael Faraday discovered that electricity can be produced when a magnet is moved inside a coil of wire. Electricity can also be produced by moving a wire wound into a coil, called an **armature**, in between two magnets.

The magnetic fields of the magnets cause electrons to move in the wire, producing electricity.

Faraday's discovery led to the development of a device called a **generator**. If you ever lose power during a storm, you'll be thankful to have a generator! Generators are devices that make electricity.

Today, most generators use an armature located between two powerful magnets to generate electricity. In a power outage, you can hook up your refrigerator to a generator and your food will stay cold!

We are lucky to live in a time when we have electricity to heat our homes, cook our food, and power our lights and appliances. Even just 100 years ago, we burned wood to cook food and heat homes, while candles or oil lamps provided light. Because of the work of scientists and other innovators, we are now able to use electricity to make life easier.

Electricity Farms

There are several types of renewable energy farms, including wind, solar, and hydroelectric power. We will see more and more of these types of farms popping up all over the United States as we reduce our dependence on fossil fuels.

In many countries in Europe, wind turbine farms account for almost 10 percent of electricity produced. In 2015, 42 percent of the electricity consumed in Denmark was produced from wind power.

A wind farm has many wind turbines in the same area. One turbine is able to provide electricity to hundreds of homes. How does electricity come from the wind?

When the wind blows it moves the blades of the wind turbine. These blades are attached to a **rotor**, which turns as the blades rotate. The rotor is attached to gears in the **gearbox** transmission. Rotation of the blades and rotor turn gears in the gearbox, creating mechanical energy.

Did You Know?

Anemometers are instruments devised hundreds of years ago to measure wind speed and pressure. The word *anemometer* comes from the Greek word *anemos*, which means "wind." The average wind speed is determined by counting the number of complete turns the anemometer makes.

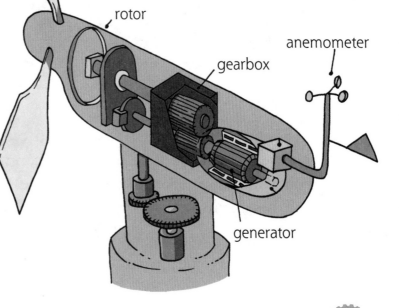

blades

rotor

gearbox

anemometer

generator

31

Bioengineering

silicon: an element used in solar panels that can interact with photons to release electrons.

element: a substance whose atoms are all the same. Examples of elements include gold, oxygen, and carbon.

photon: a particle of energy in sunlight.

toxic: something that is poisonous or harmful.

photosynthesis: the process through which plants create food, using light as a source of energy.

WORDS TO KNOW

The mechanical energy received from the gearbox turns the armature between the two magnets located in the generator. The movement of the armature within the magnetic field makes the electrons in the wire travel out of the generator as electricity.

Another way to harvest energy is through the use of solar panels. Solar panels can be found on houses, businesses, and on solar farms all across the world. Solar panels contain **silicon**. This **element** makes electricity by interacting with the **photons** that make up the sunlight that streams down to our planet.

sunlight

Photons enter the solar panel and cause a molecule of silicon to release an electron. If a bunch of silicon molecules releases electrons, you get a flow of electrons from the solar panel. This electricity can be stored for later or used right away.

The manufacturing of solar panels produces some **toxic** waste. What if we could invent a solar panel that was cleaner to produce?

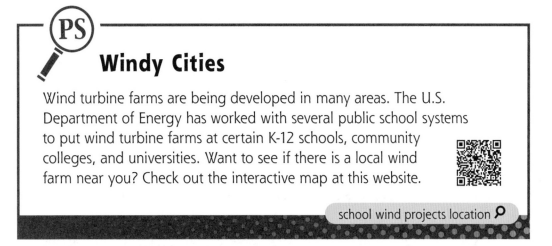

PS

Windy Cities

Wind turbine farms are being developed in many areas. The U.S. Department of Energy has worked with several public school systems to put wind turbine farms at certain K-12 schools, community colleges, and universities. Want to see if there is a local wind farm near you? Check out the interactive map at this website.

school wind projects location 🔍

Bioengineers are looking for ways to make solar panels more efficient and environmentally friendly. Biomimetic bioengineers are creating solar panels out of plants! Leaves are natural solar panels. Using **photosynthesis**, leaves of plants and trees convert sunlight into their own food. Researchers have discovered that they can harvest the chemical plants use for photosynthesis and change it to produce an electric current when the sun hits it on a solar panel. Can you think of other ways we can use nature to harvest energy?

Hydroelectric power is another renewable resource that can generate electricity. Right now, 7 percent of electricity in the United States is supplied by hydroelectric power. Just as with wind power, hydropower produces electricity by turning a rotor and converting this mechanical energy into electrical energy. Instead of using wind to move the blades, hydroelectric power uses water.

When water flows downhill, either because of the natural flow of a river or because of a dam, the water can be directed through a water turbine. The water spins the blades, setting off the chain reaction that makes electricity.

? **ESSENTIAL QUESTION**

Now it's time to consider and discuss the Essential Question: How does bioengineering help us get the electrical energy we need?

Electrifying Electroscopes

IDEAS FOR SUPPLIES
plastic bottle • paper clip • aluminum foil
• clay or playdough or duct tape • balloon

Electrons are so tiny that you can't see them with just your eyes. But you can see static electricity and electrons flowing with an electroscope.

1 Have an adult help you cut across the plastic bottle in two places. Cut at the top where the bottle begins to taper, and about an inch from the bottom. Place the top piece into the bottom piece for this activity.

2 Unbend a paper clip so that it is straight, with a small hook on the bottom. Drape a piece of aluminum foil over the hook of the paper clip.

3 Roll a ball of clay or playdough and poke the straight part of the paper clip through the clay ball so that enough is peeking through the other side that you can hold it.

4 Place the aluminum foil and hook through the top of the bottle and lower it. Stop once the ball of clay covers the opening.

WORDS TO KNOW

friction: the rubbing of one object against another. Also the force that resists motion between two objects in contact.

5 Blow up a balloon, tie it, and rub it against the top of your head. When the balloon has built up enough negative charge from the **friction**, it will stick to the wall.

ACTIVITY

6 Once the balloon is charged, place the charged area near the piece of paper clip sticking out of the clay. What happens to the aluminum foil inside the bottle? Why? Can you tell which way the electron flow is occurring?

THINK MORE: What does static electricity do to other types of matter? Open the electroscope and put 4 tablespoons of salt on the bottom of the bottle. Sprinkle 1 teaspoon of pepper on top of the salt. What happens to the pepper in the bottom of the electroscope? What is happening to the salt? You can try this experiment with other dry ingredients, such as baking soda and cinnamon. What happens?

Design an electroscope that can pick up heavier matter. What changes do you need to make? What materials could you try? Record your ideas in your bioengineering journal and design a new prototype following the engineering design principles.

Make an Anemometer

1-liter soda bottle • 4 smaller water bottles
• 2 caps from bottles • popsicle sticks

An anemometer is an instrument that measures wind speed and pressure. Although we cannot make a device that measures wind pressure, we can make one that measures average wind speed.

Caution: An adult must help you to make holes in the bottle caps.

1 Cut out the middle part of the soda bottle and put to the side. Cut the bottoms off of the four water bottles and place to the side.

2 Glue a bottle cap inside the bottom portion of the soda bottle. Put some small rocks around the bottle cap so that the anemometer will have a little weight.

3 Put the tapered top into the bottom so that it is now a miniature version of a soda bottle. You might have to squeeze it in.

4 Have an adult help you cut a hole into a soda bottle cap, large enough for a pencil to turn freely. Twist the bottle cap tightly onto the soda bottle opening.

5 Sharpen a new pencil. Glue four popsicle sticks near the eraser in a circular pattern as seen in the picture. After the glue has dried, glue a water bottle bottom onto each popsicle stick as shown.

ACTIVITY

6 Color one of the water bottle bottoms with a sharpie or put masking tape on it. Why do you think this is important?

7 Once your anemometer is up and running, go use it! Watch the number of rotations that your anemometer makes. Using a timer, count the number of times the colored bottle bottom makes a complete revolution in one minute.

8 Average wind speed is measured in revolutions, or turns, per minute. At a weather station, a scientist will convert the revolutions per minute into miles per hour. How would you convert the revolutions per minute to revolutions per hour? Remember, there are 60 minutes in an hour!

THINK MORE: If an anemometer makes 10 rotations in 10 minutes, how many miles per hour is the average wind speed?

Design a Wind Turbine

IDEAS FOR SUPPLIES

anemometer from previous activity • *popsicle sticks* • *pencils* •
water bottle and cap • *straw* • *string with spool* • *balloon*

Use part of your anemometer for this project. Remove the pencil with the glued bottle bottoms and place to the side. Use the rest of the anemometer to make different wind turbine models.

> **Caution:** An adult must help you to make holes in the bottle caps.

1 Remember, a wind turbine uses the force of the wind to create mechanical energy that accomplishes work. You need to create blades and a rotor for your wind turbine to do the same thing. What will your goal be?
Do you want to lift or move something with the mechanical energy created by your wind turbine?

2 Make a wind turbine like the one in the picture. How will you make the string wrap around the spool using just wind? Is the turbine strong enough to lift a weight on the other end of the string? Try it!

3 Design a different wind turbine using these or other materials. Can you think of better things to use as blades? How can you design it so it will produce stronger mechanical energy? Can you make a turbine that is more efficient and more useful?

THINK MORE: What can you find in nature that inspires you to improve your design? Keep track of your ideas and results in your engineering journal. Make prototypes using your different designs.

Fish-Inspired Wind Turbines

One recent development in wind power has been modeling wind turbines based on the dynamics seen in a school of swimming fish. Biophysicist Dr. John Dabiri discovered that if vertical wind turbines are clustered close together, each turbine could benefit from the breeze coming off the turbines around them. This biomimetic approach results in smaller, more efficient wind turbines.

fish-inspired wind farms 🔎

Chapter 3

BIOENGINEERED HOUSEHOLD

Some objects in your house have been designed by people who studied nature. Did you grow up wearing shoes that used Velcro instead of shoe laces? Bioengineers have many ideas to use nature to solve problems around the house.

How about a strong **adhesive** that peels off easily when you want it to? How about rechargeable batteries that last a long time and are safe for the environment? While many more ideas are still in the prototype stage, some products are available for your home right now. What is the first thing you think of when you hear the word *adhesive*? Glue? Tape? How about gecko feet?

Great Gecko!

Today, some of the most powerful adhesives are being developed based on the adhesive properties of gecko feet. It might take a few years before these products reach stores near you, but bioengineers are researching ways to make gecko feet adhesive useful in tough situations, such as at construction sites or in space.

WORDS TO KNOW

? ESSENTIAL QUESTION

What products do you use in your home that were inspired by nature?

To see how scientists arrived at the idea of using gecko feet as a model for developing powerful adhesive, let's take a look at what geckos can do. Geckos can climb on glass walls at about 40 inches per second, which is equivalent to 80 miles per hour. They can hang upside down on a glass surface and support an object that weighs 50 times their own body weight.

How do geckos accomplish these amazing feats? Gecko feet have millions of little hairs called setae. On each end of those millions of hairs are thousands of plates called spatulae. At the microscopic level, the setae can stick to anything by using the right mechanics and chemistry.

All matter, including gecko feet, is made of atoms. You learned in the last chapter that an atom has electrons with a negative charge, neutrons with no charge, and protons with a positive charge.

Remember the rules of charges? Like charges repulse each other, but opposite charges are attracted to each other. An atom that has an area of temporary positive charge will be attracted to another atom that has an area of negative charge.

Try This!

What do you think Leonardo da Vinci meant when he said, "Human ingenuity may make various inventions, but it will never devise any inventions more beautiful, nor more simple, nor more to the purpose than Nature does; because in her inventions nothing is wanting and nothing is superfluous."

On geckos, each individual setae adheres to a surface through a temporary interaction known as a Van der Waals force. Van der Waals forces work because the charged areas of atoms on the setae are attracted to the charged areas of whatever surface the gecko is climbing. This interaction is very weak and normally doesn't need a lot of force to break it.

But while the strength in the interaction between one setae and the wall might be very tiny, you have several million Van de Waals interactions happening all at once. That adds up to a lot of strength! This is why a gecko can hold its own weight and an additional object 50 times its weight while upside down.

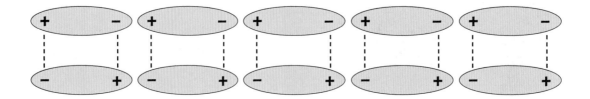

Geckos Use the Force!

An atom can have a fleeting charge based on where its charged particles are. It might be helpful to think of an atom as a cloud with its electrons being able to move within it. If all the electrons move to the left side of the cloud, what will the overall charge be at that side, positive or negative? How about on the right side of the cloud? These changes in charge are just temporary because the atom has not lost an electron.

If the gecko is able to make such a strong connection with the wall, how can it continue to move and not just stay put? The setae have flexibility that mechanically counteracts the Van der Waals force.

When the angle of the setae changes with respect to the wall, the adhesion immediately stops. Since so little force is required to make the setae stick to a wall, the gecko can climb any wall with amazing speed.

Application of gecko adhesive in the human world is very exciting to think about.

Maybe someday, astronauts will use gecko adhesive when they perform spacewalks, so they won't have to wear bulky harnesses that tether them to the spacecraft. When construction workers have to maneuver into a dangerous spot while working on skyscrapers, gecko adhesive could help them stay safe. Can you think of other things gecko adhesive might be used for?

Bioengineering

Mussel Muscles

A mussel is a marine animal that lives in a shell. Mussels cling to rocks in groups underwater. How do they stick to the rocks? A mussel has an organ called a foot that can reach slightly out of its shell. A **gland** in the foot produces sticky proteins that bind together to form long, smooth threads. These threads, called byssal threads, make a strong waterproof adhesive that binds the mussel to the rock.

Scientists have begun to examine and mimic the properties of these sticky proteins. They have developed a glue based on byssal threads. It is not easy to find a glue that can work in dry and wet areas. Try using an ordinary glue stick underwater—it doesn't work! Since glue modeled on byssal threads is both strong and can work in wet environments, it would work well to glue wounds after surgery! Can you think of any other uses?

(PS) Ocean Acidification

Due to climate change and an increase in greenhouse gases, our oceans are becoming more acidic. Most living things do not like to live in either an **acidic** or a **basic** environment. Acidification of the ocean leads to another harmful process called **decalcification**. During decalcification, **calcium** is removed from a substance. It is the presence of calcium that makes our bones hard.

Decalcification is bad news for all organisms that have calcium in their shells. These organisms might not be able to build shells for themselves anymore. Current research shows that the adhesive glue from mussels might be affected as well because the adhesive properties of byssal threads are lost when placed in acidic conditions. The end result is that mussels might not be able to cling to rocks. You can read more about ocean acidification and view a tracking map of the problem at this website.

NOAA ocean acidification 🔍

Clean Your Room!

What if everything in your house were self-cleaning? Does this sound too good to be true? We might not be that far away from having self-cleaning technology in our homes, schools, and businesses!

Lotus plants often live in muddy water, but they are never dirty. This is sometimes called the *lotus effect*, and is due to the top side of the lotus leaf having lots of **papillae** on its surface. Wax tubules and wax clusters surround the papillae.

Try This!

If you go to a mirror and stick out your tongue, you will see that it is covered with papillae! The function of our papillae is to assist with taste, as most papillae on our tongue have taste buds.

The papillae on lotus leaves have a different function from the papillae on your tongue. The effect of the waxy papillae on lotus leaves is to create a super **hydrophobic** surface that water doesn't cling to well.

The prefix *hydro* comes from the Greek word for "water" and *phobic* comes from the Greek word for "fear." The wax-covered surface makes the leaf hydrophobic. Water droplets tend to adhere to other water droplets, but cannot adhere to fatty molecules such as wax.

What happens when you pour oil into a glass of water? Both liquids like to adhere to themselves, but they don't mix well together. The same thing happens on a lotus plant.

Dirt will not adhere to wax, but will easily mix with any water. Therefore, when it rains, water droplets bead together to form larger water drops. These water drops take any dirt in their path and fall off the leaf.

Other plants have leaves that are hydrophobic as well, but the papillae on the lotus leaf make it the best at self-cleaning.

Some clothes, cars, and paint have been manufactured to have this self-cleaning ability. Self-cleaning clothes are made from cloth that contains long cotton fibers with silicone or another hydrophobic substance added to them. This produces the bumps and the hydrophobic surface that lotus leaves possess. These shirts have been shown to shrug off staining substances, such as coffee, ketchup, and wine. Can you think of other objects that could benefit from the ability to self-clean?

Viral Batteries

Try This!

Place a teaspoon of baking soda in a glass and then add some vinegar. What happens? The baking soda and vinegar are reacting to each other in a chemical reaction.

How many batteries do you go through in your house? Most houses have lots of batteries in many different devices, such as remote controls, gaming controllers, flashlights, and smoke alarms.

A battery is a device that produces electricity through several chemical reactions. A chemical reaction is when two or more chemicals interact and chemically change. You have seen plenty of chemical reactions, but you might not have known it. For example, if you were to mix vinegar and baking soda together, the bubbling you see is the result of a chemical reaction.

The first type of battery consisted of the metals copper and zinc, plus an **electrolyte solution**. Even though batteries have changed significantly since the first one was made in 1800, the way they work has stayed pretty much the same.

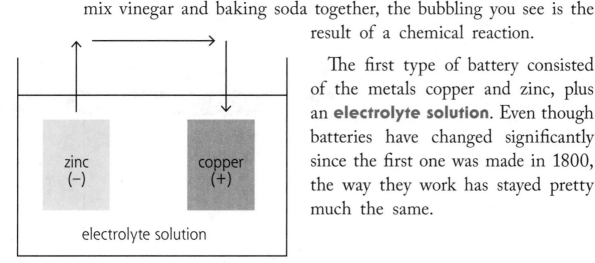

zinc (−)

copper (+)

electrolyte solution

Bioengineering

One metal likes to "lose" electrons and another metal likes to "gain" electrons. During the chemical reaction within a battery, a stockpile of ions builds up. Once a battery is placed in a device, the electrons have somewhere to go and their movement, or electric charge, powers the device!

Once all the chemicals have been used up, no more chemical reactions can occur. If the battery isn't rechargeable, it stops working.

Right now, the most powerful and long-lasting battery is a lithium-ion battery. These are not easy to manufacture. They also contain toxic chemicals, which means you can't just throw them out.

Bioengineers at Dr. Angela Belcher's laboratory at Massachusetts Institute of Technology are using **viruses** to develop a battery that lasts longer, is safer to manufacture, and is much more environmentally friendly. A virus is a non-living microbe that normally has only two goals—to make more of itself and to find a new host to infect. People get sick from some viruses, including the flu virus, every year.

The virus that bioengineers use in batteries only infects certain **bacteria**. It is completely harmless to people. The virus works by attaching metal to itself and forming an intricate network of tubes. This large network allows electricity to be quickly transferred. Rechargeable batteries made with the M13 virus have a flexible shape and might be able to power many devices, including cars!

? ESSENTIAL QUESTION

Now it's time to consider and discuss the Essential Question: What products do you use in your home that were inspired by nature?

Lovely Lotus Leaves!

IDEAS FOR SUPPLIES

*leaf of lettuce • leaf of kale • spray bottle filled with water
• very dry dirt • engineering journal and pencil*

In this activity, you will examine and compare some hydrophobic leaves and some not-so-hydrophobic leaves.

1 Spray both leaves with some water. What happens to the droplets of water? Why?

2 Immerse each leaf in a bowl full of water. What does each leaf look like underwater? Now take both leaves out of the water. Which leaf appears to be drier? Why do you think that is?

3 Shake some very dry, loose dirt on each leaf. Spray again with water and observe which leaf is cleaner after this treatment. Which leaf behaves more like the lotus leaves that we discussed in this chapter? Look at the cleaner leaf closely. What properties does the leaf have that make it hydrophobic? What else can you do to test and compare your leaves?

THINK MORE: What devices would benefit from being able to self-clean? Design a self-cleaning device that fulfills a need. Would people use your device for medical reasons? Entertainment? Travel? How would you keep your device self-cleaning during long periods of time? How would you make it cost-effective to produce? Record your design ideas in your design notebook.

Make Your Own Glue

water • 2 tablespoons corn syrup • 1 teaspoon vinegar • 2 tablespoons cornstarch

You can make your own glue using just a few common ingredients from the pantry. Use the following recipe to make glue, and then think of your own recipe using what you know about the ingredients you choose!

Caution: An adult must help you handle the hot liquids.

1 Measure a ½ cup of tap water into a microwavable bowl or cup with a handle. Add corn syrup and vinegar to the bowl and mix well with a whisk.

2 Microwave the bowl for 1 minute, until the contents are boiling. Have a parent remove the hot container from the microwave.

3 In the meantime, prepare another ½ cup of water in a measuring cup and add cornstarch. Mix well with a whisk.

4 Slowly add the cornstarch mixture into the corn syrup mixture with a whisk. Place back in the microwave and cook for 1½ minutes.

Try This!

Now try making your own recipe for glue! What will you use for ingredients? Will you heat your glue or can you make it cold? What process works best? Find a recipe that works and record your attempts in your engineering design journal!

5 Have a parent remove the hot bowl from the microwave. Set aside for a few minutes to cool and then place in a sealable container for a few hours at room temperature before use.

ACTIVITY

50

Transportation has held people's imagination for a long time. Humans want choices in how they get from place to place around the world. They want to be able to go to their destinations quickly, smoothly, and soundlessly. And, of course, everyone wants their transportation to look good!

? ESSENTIAL QUESTION

Move It!

When engineers design a new kind of car, airplane, train, or other vehicle, they have to consider the basic laws of physics. These laws dictate how **forces** and motion work.

Sir Isaac Newton is the scientist credited with describing the three laws of motion. He lived in England in the 1600s and is considered to be the "Father of Physics." Newton was the first person to describe the concept of **gravity**, which is the invisible force that pulls everything together. Gravity is the reason we can walk around on the earth and not float off into space. Newton read many books, but he also believed in observing nature.

Legend has it that Sir Isaac Newton came up with the idea of gravity while watching an apple fall from a tree.

Newton's first law of motion states that "a stationary body will stay stationary unless an external force is applied to it" and "an object in motion will tend to stay in motion until an external force is applied to it." This means, if you leave an apple on a table, the apple should still be in the same spot later unless someone or something moves it.

Newton's first law of motion
A stationary body will stay stationary unless
an external force is applied to it.

The second half of Newton's first law refers to an object that is in motion. Someone or something has to apply enough force to an object to make it move. The object will continue to move until an outside force acts on it to make it stop. If you roll a toy car down a ramp, it will move down the ramp until you put your hand down in front of it to stop it. In this case, you provide the force.

What if you don't stop it? A toy car will eventually stop without your help. Perhaps it will slam into a wall or roll onto a thick carpet. The carpet will stop it with the force of friction, which is what happens when two objects rub against each other.

Newton's second law of motion states, "Force is equal to **mass** times **acceleration**, and a change in motion is proportional to the force applied." Acceleration is a change in speed or direction. To make something move faster, we need to apply more force. Do you need more or less force to get a larger mass accelerating? If you are pulling a wagon with your younger brother in it and your friend jumps in, do you have to use more or less force to move the wagon at the same speed?

Did You Know?

Sports offer lots of opportunities to learn about Newton's laws of motion! Watch this video on hockey.

Newton's laws and hockey 🔍

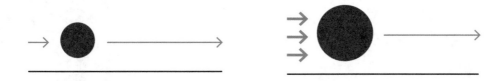

Newton's second law of motion
Force is equal to mass times acceleration, and a change in motion is proportional to the force applied.
$F = ma$

Bioengineering

Newton's third law of motion states, "For every action there is an equal and opposite reaction." This means that if one object exerts a force on a second object, then the second object also exerts an opposite force on the first object. Both of these forces are equal and will result in both objects not moving. For example, the chair that you are sitting on right now is exerting a force that is counteracting the force of your weight.

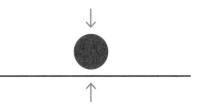

Newton's third law of motion
For every action there is an equal and opposite reaction.

For movement to occur, there needs to be an unbalanced amount of force. If you and a friend are playing tug of war and another person joins your friend on the other side of the rope, who's going to win? That's an unbalanced force!

Bioengineers use these laws of motion when they design new processes or devices.

Look Up!

For the past two thousand years, individuals have designed flying devices based on the bodies and behaviors of birds and bats. Most early attempts at human flight were unsuccessful. Sadly, many people died trying to fly like birds.

In the 1400s, Leonardo da Vinci designed a number of flying machines, including the ornithopter and helicopter. These flying machines were based on his observations of birds and bats. His illustrations are an example of biomimetics at its best.

Da Vinci watched how birds moved in the air. He examined their skeletal structure, especially the wings. The wings he designed for his machines were very similar to the structure of bird wings. Some of his drawings show that he was thinking about adding mechanics to his machines that would allow the pilot to power the wings in a manner similar to birds'.

It is unknown how many of da Vinci's designs were built, but there was an entry in his notebooks of a failed flight. You can find a link to his notebooks on page 6.

The Father of Flying Models

Alphonse Pénaud (1850–1880) has been called the "Father of Flying Models." He built a number of rubber-band-driven propeller models, called planophores, as well as ornithopters and helicopters. His designs were influenced by birds and bats. In 1871, he flew a planophore 181 feet in 11 seconds! He wanted to build a full-sized flying machine based on his toy models, but wasn't able to raise the money to do so.

Hundreds of years later one of da Vinci's flight machines was built to his specifications. The materials used were only those that would have been available to him, and it had a successful flight!

The Wright Brothers

Two men who used the laws of motion to reach great heights were Orville and Wilbur Wright. The Wright brothers were encouraged from an early age to design, improve, and experiment with any toy or instrument that they encountered. Their mother, who was mechanically inclined, made several of their toys.

The brothers were quite opposite in personality. Wilbur was quiet, studious, and thoughtful, while Orville was energetic, optimistic, and an endless tinkerer. Together, they **complemented** each other. They might not have been able to achieve as much alone as they did working together.

Did You Know?

In 1000 BCE, the Chinese invented kites that could carry men.

In 1887, bicycles were all the rage. Since Wilbur and Orville had a reputation for fixing and tinkering with items, the neighbors asked them to fix their broken bikes. Realizing that they could make a living by fixing bicycles, the brothers opened a bike shop. They rented and repaired bikes and eventually manufactured some of their own design.

After a few years of running their bike shop, they began experimenting in the field of aviation.

The brothers used some of the key elements of their bicycle design first in the design of their **gliders** and eventually in the creation of a flying machine. Both bicycles and flying machines require strong, low-weight materials, centralized balance features, **aerodynamic** design, and a chain-and-sprocket transmission system.

The Wright brothers understood that there are four different forces that work on airplanes in motion. To build a machine that would fly, the brothers had to take all four forces into consideration—weight, **thrust**, **lift**, and **drag**.

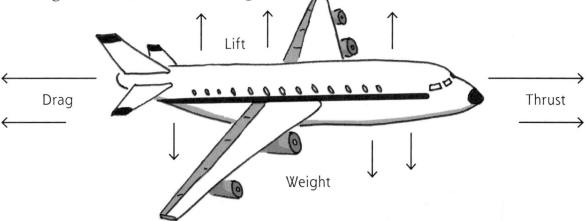

Airplanes have a certain weight, which is caused by gravity acting on the plane's mass. This force works against getting a plane into the air. Thrust is a force that propels an object forward. In the case of an airplane, the force of thrust is provided by the engines.

Lift propels a plane vertically upward and is achieved once a plane has reached about 150 to 180 miles per hour. The wing design and the speed of the air across the surfaces of the wings create lower pressure on top of the wing and higher pressure on the bottom of the wing. That high pressure creates an unbalanced force and pushes the plane into the air.

The forces of lift and thrust must be greater than the weight of the plane for it to rise. There must be quite a lot of lift and thrust to get a commercial plane into the air. It can weigh anywhere from 100,000 to 900,000 pounds!

Drag is the final force that affects an airplane. Drag is caused by friction between the air and the surface of the object. When air hits an object's surface, it pushes against the surface. To limit the amount of drag, planes are designed to be aerodynamic.

The forces of lift and gravity oppose each other and the forces of thrust and drag oppose each other.

The Wright brothers reasoned that it made sense to first test a glider. Just as Leonardo da Vinci had done, the brothers used biomimetics to observe and learn how birds fly in nature. Wilbur and Orville observed pigeons during flight and noticed that they made slight adjustments with both wings while making a turn. The brothers believed that their glider needed flexible, curved wings that would allow them also to make adjustments during flight.

PS Doing Things the Wright Way!

Orville and Wilbur Wright loved to tinker. Their method of building a prototype, collecting test-run data, and redesigning a new prototype based on the data they'd collected is largely the way engineering projects are conducted now.

You can see the Wright brothers doing a test flight with their flying machines. How is their airplane different from the planes we fly today? What improvements have been made to make the machines safer?

Wright brothers test flight video 🔍

Try This!

Build a model airplane and see how the four forces affect it. You can find design ideas at this website.

how things fly forces 🔍

Other engineers thought that the wing shape should be curved, with the highest point of the curve in the middle of the wing. But Orville and Wilbur Wright determined that it needed to be at the highest point, toward the end of the wing.

In 1900, the Wright brothers made their first glider prototype. A glider can be flown using a rope or it can be piloted by a person inside the glider. They tested their glider in the town of Kitty Hawk, a very windy area on an island off the coast of North Carolina.

Their first glider did not perform very well, but they returned to their hometown of Dayton, Ohio, undaunted. In 1901, they built another glider prototype with adjustments based on their previous test runs in Kitty Hawk. Unfortunately, the 1901 glider had even more problems, particularly with achieving lift. They decided to build a wind tunnel in which they tested about 50 different wing types out of the 200 they had made.

After lots of testing, they built a final glider in 1902. This glider was a tremendous success and served as a model for the production of their first powered aircraft, named *Flyer*. The Wrights designed their first aircraft by altering some key components to compensate for the added weight of an engine, propellers, and additional structural components. On December 17, 1903, Wilbur and Orville Wright made history with four short flights at Kitty Hawk with *Flyer*.

(PS)

Maple Seed Drone

A company recently designed a motorized drone based on the aerodynamics of maple seeds. Maple seeds need to travel far from their trees to find good places to grow into new maple trees. You can see the maple seed drone in action here.

Samarai maple seed 🔍

Other Forms of Transportation

Many forms of transportation, including cars and trains, also have designs that have been influenced by nature. When engineers in Japan wanted to solve the problem of the sonic boom that happened any time a high-speed train emerged from a tunnel, they looked to nature for ideas. How could they change the shape of the train so it moved through the air more quietly?

The kingfisher bird can enter the water in search of a meal and hardly make a ripple. Taking inspiration from the bird, engineers designed a bullet train that was built with a nose like the beak of a kingfisher bird. The result? A much more quiet, fuel-efficient, faster train!

What other transportation problems can be solved by using biomimetics?

? **ESSENTIAL QUESTION**

Now it's time to consider and discuss the Essential Question: If you were designing a car, where in nature would you look for ideas?

Maple Seed Flight

IDEAS FOR SUPPLIES
paper • scissors • glue

The maple seed generates a lot of lift and spirals when falling. In this activity, you'll make your own maple seeds and observe how they move.

1 Draw your own maple seeds based on the illustration and cut them out.

2 Think about the question, "What makes the maple seed move in a spiraling motion?" In your engineering journal, write down some things that you think are important to flight based on your reading of this chapter. What did the Wright brothers notice?

3 Stand on a stool or chair and hold a paper maple seed by the wing and drop it straight down. Do you notice any circular movement? The spiraling movement relies on the three-dimensional shape of the maple seed. Your paper seed is two dimensional. How might this affect the seed's fall?

4 Brainstorm changes you can make to the paper maple seed to make it more likely to experience lift and circular movement. Try folding, bending, cutting, and adding weight. Record your changes in your journal.

THINK MORE: Test your new designs. Do any of them spin to the ground like real maple seeds? Can you improve on the natural design? What use might these maple seed designs have in your daily life?

Rubber Band-Powered Helicopter

IDEAS FOR SUPPLIES

2 plastic water bottles with caps • 2 paper clips • 4 straws • wing template from nomadpress.net/templates • 1 rubber band • paper • glue

Alphonse Pénaud made rubber-band-powered flight machines in the 1800s. Try to make your own rubber band model that is based on his inventions.

Caution: An adult must help you to make holes in the bottle caps.

1 Using scissors, make a small hole in the center of each of the bottle caps. Unwind both paper clips so each has a hook on one end and is straight on the other end.

2 Cut the top spout and the bottom portion off of both plastic bottles. Take the middle part of each bottle and cut it lengthwise into two equal strips. You should have a total of four equal pieces.

3 Print out four copies of the bat wing (nomadpress.net/templates) and cut them out. Glue one bat wing on to one bottle piece so that the paper wing follows the curve of the bottle to make curved wings.

4 To make the structure of the helicopter, cut two of the straws in half. Take two of the halves and find the middle of each. Measure about an inch around the middle and fold each side of the straw down on both straws. Take the remaining straight straw halves and interlock them by pinching one end of a straw and putting it in the other. If the straws don't stay interlocked, you can add some glue to the end of the straw that is being placed inside the other straw. Complete this so that you have a rectangle.

5 Have a parent poke a hole through the middle of each of the short sides of the rectangle. Cut four 1-inch pieces off of a new straw. Poke a hole through the middle of these straws as well. Cut the last straw in half. Put the straight part of one paper clip through the small side of the rectangle, then through the bottle cap, then through two of the 1-inch straw pieces and finally twist it around one ½ straw piece as seen in the picture. Do the same on the other side. The hook should be on the inside of the rectangle structure.

6 Glue one wing on each side of both straws (four wings total). Glue them so that one wing is curving up on one side and the other wing is curving downward on the other side as shown in the picture.

7 Take the rubber band and loop it around each of the two paper clip hooks to finish your helicopter. Hold one end and twist the other end until you have put a lot of twists and tension in the rubber band. Hold your helicopter in the middle and let the top and bottom propellers go! Are they turning in the same direction? Why not?

THINK MORE: Apply some more engineering design to your project! Can you think of some other materials or design changes that would help your helicopter stay suspended in the air? Keep track of your ideas in your engineering notebook!

Paper Airplanes

IDEAS FOR SUPPLIES
*paper airplane template from nomadpress.net/templates •
paper • tape • measuring tape*

In 2011, about 22 miles above Wolfsburg, Germany, 100 paper airplanes were released. They traveled as far as the United States, Canada, and Russia! In this project, you'll follow instructions to build a paper airplane, then use what you have observed about birds and other creatures that fly and glide to improve the design.

1 Print and cut out the color paper airplane template from nomadpress.net/templates.

2 Fold in half once horizontally and unfold. Now turn over the paper and fold the yellow corners to the center line.

3 Now take the ends of each triangle and fold to the center line again. Your airplane should look like the picture to the far right.

4 With the colored side facing up, there are three lines running through the green section in the middle. Fold and unfold along the outside lines. Then fold in half along the center line and reverse the outside folds.

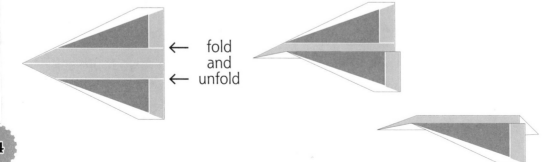

← fold
and
← unfold

5 Lastly, from the color side fold back a ½ inch of paper on the outside edge of both wings.

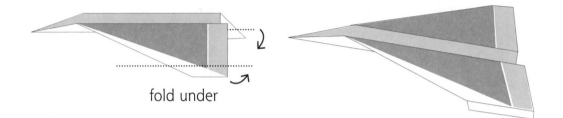

fold under

6 Now fly your plane! Do several test runs and measure how far the plane goes each time. To find the average run, add up all of your distances and divide that number by the number of test runs you made.

For example, say you made four test runs with the following results.

★ Test run #1 = 16 feet   ★ Test run #3 = 20 feet

★ Test run #2 = 18 feet   ★ Test run #4 = 12 feet

Your equation would look like this:
$(16 + 18 + 20 + 12) \div 4 =$ **16.5 feet is the average run**

THINK MORE: Now that you have made a basic paper plane, what changes can you make to the design to make it go further? Set a goal of how far you want the plane to fly. Do some research to find other paper airplane designs that have flown well. Are there any common design elements? Sketch some designs in your design notebook and then build your prototypes. What will you change to make your airplane fly farther? Keep track of all the changes and test results in your notebook. What is the best design you can come up with?

Chapter 5

CONSTRUCTION AND ARCHITECTURE

Some architects use biomimetics to design buildings by applying nature's blueprints. For example, insects have been building homes much longer than humans—why not learn from the experts?

Architects, whether they are people or insects, have to rely on the principles of physics when constructing a house. They need to be sure the force of the building is equal to the forces applied against the building, so the building doesn't tumble to the ground. Can you imagine if they didn't rely on the principles of physics? The Eiffel Tower would no longer be standing tall, it would be a pile of rubble on the ground.

The First Steps

A building must face many things, including wind, earthquakes, heavy snow, and an environment that can be dry, wet, hot, cold, or acidic. These are all things an architect must take into consideration when designing a house. Of course, they also have to deal with gravity! Can you think of some more factors that affect a building?

Not only does a building have to survive external forces, it also has to survive use by the inhabitants. At the same time it must keep them safe and comfortable.

Before starting to build, you must look at the surrounding environment. A building needs a solid **foundation** to rest upon. Do you remember Newton's third law of motion, which states that for every action there is an opposite and equal reaction? How does this apply to a building's foundation?

What happens when a building doesn't have a good foundation? Look no further than the Leaning Tower of Pisa! Built about 1360, the tower started to lean during construction because the foundation was too soft.

blueprint: a design for a building.

foundation: the base of a home or other building that is partly underground. The foundation supports the weight of the building.

WORDS TO KNOW

? ESSENTIAL QUESTION

If you were designing a house inspired by nature, what elements would you include?

Bioengineering

In addition to the foundation needing to be able to support the weight of the building, a building needs to have a structural frame supported by **load-bearing** walls. This means that the walls are capable of holding weight.

Equally important is the type of materials used to build the structure. Remember the fairy tale about the three little pigs? Those pigs had no luck living in houses made of sticks and straw, but bricks were certainly useful! Concrete is fire-resistant and a useful material to build a housing structure. What other materials would be good choices to use in the building process?

Often, a building needs to be designed to serve a certain purpose. A house might have a different design from a school, and an apartment building will be different from an airport. Architects consider these needs when they are designing new structures.

There are many types of design elements that can serve a purpose in a building. For example, a **cantilever** is a beam or structure that juts out of a building in mid-air. It almost appears to be supported by an invisible hook from the sky. The cantilever is supported on one end and is able to bear a load on the opposite end without support.

The Physics of Cantilever Bridges

Cantilevers are used for bridges as well as buildings. You can learn more about this design element at this website.

firth of Forth bridge PBS learning media 🔍

Architectural design has long been influenced by nature. In the past, though, architects were simply inspired to include decorations, such as leaves or flowers, as part of the design. Nature is more and more considered to be integral to the whole design process. One way this happens is through **organic architecture**, a term first used by architect Frank Lloyd Wright.

Try This!

Frank Lloyd Wright said, on nature-inspired design, "This is what nature produces. These shells all are based on the same basic principles, but all of them are different, and they're all created as a function of the interior use of that shell." What did he mean by this? How do different designs come as a result of one need?

Organic architecture is when the surrounding nature is pulled into and remains part of the final building design. Frank Lloyd Wright made structures within his buildings that looked like trees or lily pads. Biomimetics takes organic architecture one step further by incorporating ways in which the natural world functions as well as what it looks like.

Ideas From Creatures

Nature offers design solutions that architects have recently been using to design buildings. For example, how do termites stay cool even in the heat? Termite mounds are able to maintain a moderate internal temperature even when it's extremely hot outside.

Bioengineering

Termite mounds are tall, with a main shaft that seems to circulate hot and cool air within the mound. Because of this, the temperature is relatively constant year-round. The mound is made of saliva and feces from the termites, combined with dirt. While the material is not ideal for use in building houses for humans, the design of the mound is!

An architect from Zimbabwe designed an office building based on the termite mound.

This biomimetically designed building saves money on heating and cooling bills because the internal temperature is able to stay relatively constant despite temperature changes outside.

While the thought of a sponge evokes the thought of something squishy, sea sponges are anything but! The humble but strong sea sponge has been the object of much scientific study. Several sea sponges have skeletons made of glass material that are unbreakable, even when stepped on!

Bacterial Builders

Bricks, concrete slabs, metal, wood, plastic, and cement are some of the materials used to construct buildings. One problem with these building materials is that many are not **biodegradable** and eventually end up in our **landfills**. While the termites have taken biodegradable building materials to a new level by combining spit with dirt and feces, this really doesn't seem like a house people might like to live in!

Engineers and scientists have been developing new biodegradable construction materials. Bricks can be made from sand and bacteria, which is found naturally in the environment, or they can be made from minced corn husks and mushrooms. Both types of bricks are biodegradable and require few chemicals to make. Would you live in a house made using either of these types of bricks?

The Gherkin building in London is inspired by the architectural design of the Venus' flower basket sea sponge. The **exoskeleton** of this type of sponge consists of adhered layers of glass that form a grid-like, or **lattice**, design. Usually, glass is formed at super-high temperatures, so it remains a mystery as to how these sea sponges make their skeleton out of glass. The Gherkin building has this type of lattice design on its surface, which makes it a very strong building.

The building also borrows from the sea sponge the technique of filtering water up through its walls. Instead of water, though, the building filters air, which cuts way down on the air conditioning bill and makes this building very environmentally friendly.

? **ESSENTIAL QUESTION**

Now it's time to consider and discuss the **Essential Question:** If you were designing a house inspired by nature, what elements would you include?

71

Make a Termite Den!

IDEAS FOR SUPPLIES
small box • clay or homemade playdough • balloon • straw, cut in half • paper towel roll, cut in half • scissors

Termite mounds provide amazing temperature stability during temperature fluctuations. Recently, an architect used a termite mound as inspiration when designing an office building in Zimbabwe. In this activity, you'll design your own cool termite den.

1 Cut the small box in half. Place a foundation of clay in the box that is larger than the circumference of your hand.

2 Blow up a balloon to the size of your hand. Place the balloon on top of the foundation of clay.

3 Make two holes on opposite sides of the cardboard tube and place half a straw in each hole. Now hold the cardboard tube on top of the balloon with one hand and with the other hand put enough clay to completely cover the balloon and cardboard tube. Do not seal off the top of the cardboard tube or straws—these are ventilation shafts for your termite house.

4 Cover the entire bottom of the box with a thick layer of clay or playdough. Make the layer at least an inch high.

5 Let the termite house dry for several days. Once dry, pop the balloon and remove it if possible. Your termite den is ready for habitation!

ACTIVITY

6 Now design a larger termite den. You might want to build it outside! What will you use for materials? Will you create the entire mound at once or will you add a little more material to the mound each day? How will you keep it safe from animals or other people?

7 Once you have a large termite mound, test to see if the inside is cooler than the outside by placing one ice cube inside the mound and another outside the mound and measuring how long it takes for each cube to melt. What is your hypothesis? What are you results?

Termites: Friend or Foe?

Termites are pretty amazing insects! They can be found just about everywhere in the world, except on Antarctica. Their colonies might consist of several hundred individuals or several million. They have been around much, much longer than humans. In some parts of the world, these insects are considered a delicacy to eat and are often used in the making of medicine! While they're beneficial to humans in these ways, they are also considered pests that can cause significant damage to buildings and crops.

Fractal Fun

IDEAS FOR SUPPLIES
pencil • engineering journal

Fractals are an ongoing pattern created by repeating a simple process over and over. They can be found everywhere in nature—snowflakes and plants are examples of fractals. Bioengineers use fractals to solve engineering problems. Let's practice finding and drawing fractals.

1 Let's draw a Koch snowflake, which is one of the earliest fractals found. Following along with the illustrations below, start by drawing an equilateral triangle. This type of triangle has three sides that are all the same length. Once you have drawn your triangle, erase the middle third of each side. Draw a new triangle, with the point facing outward, in the place of the erased line. Do this on all sides and you should have a six-pointed star in the place of your original triangle!

Try This!

Check out these videos that show the nature of fractals!

PS

fractal foundation videos 🔍

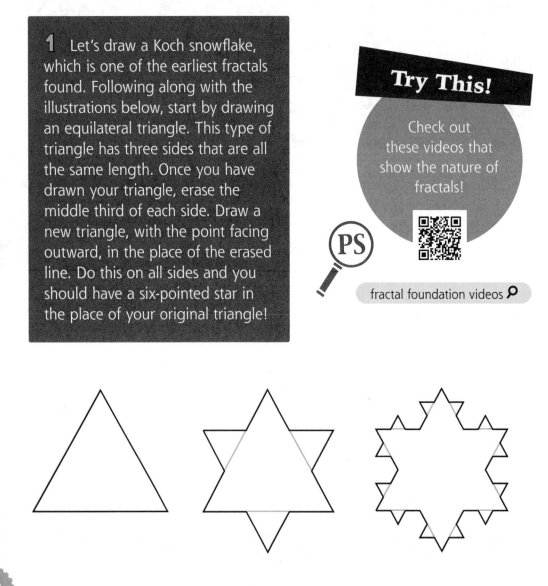

2 Now, on both sides of each of the six points (not all three sides like the last time) erase the middle part of the line. When you are finished, you should have 12 erased parts.

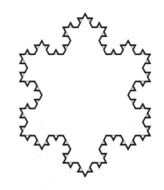

3 Now, draw a new triangle with the tip pointing out in the place of each of these erased portions. You should have 18 points now. Do this one more time. Now, how many points do you have? Does your original triangle now look more like a snowflake?

4 Let's do this with a simple tree structure. Draw a large "Y" on your page. Now, as shown in the illustration, add a wide "V" shape to each of the two top tips of the "Y." We are making the branches of the tree. Add more "V"s to each of the top tips and you will end up with a tree.

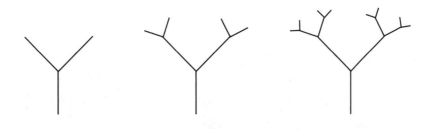

5 Go outside or look in your refrigerator for more fractals found in nature! Try to simplify each pattern to a basic shape. In your journal, expand out the simple shape into a larger fractal.

THINK MORE: Architects have long used trees as inspiration for designing buildings. How would you use a tree to build a home? Draw it in your journal and try to make a prototype from materials you have.

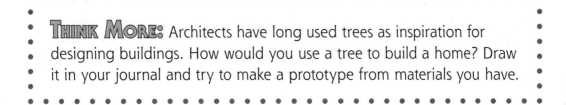

Experiment with Cantilevers

IDEAS FOR SUPPLIES

2 cups of same height • ruler • several objects of similar weight (coins, etc.)

Cantilevers are essential elements in many buildings. You can make your own model cantilevers in this activity. Find out how much weight you can support with your design!

1 Place one cup under the 6-inch mark on the ruler and the other cup under the 12-inch mark. Place weights on the 6-inch, 12-inch, and 0-inch marks. What happens to the structure? Is it stable or shaky?

2 Vary the weights that you place on the 6-inch, 12-inch, and 0-inch marks. Create a table in your design journal to record your results. Do you see a pattern? Does an uneven amount of support weight on each cup still result in a stable cantilever? Why or why not?

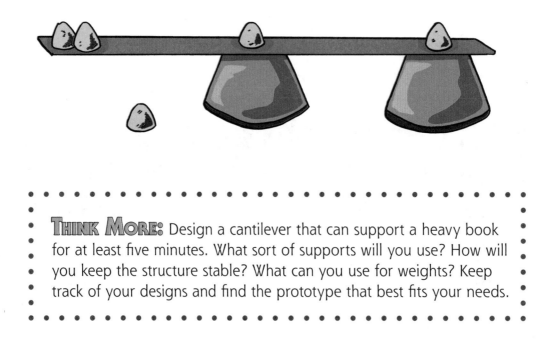

THINK MORE: Design a cantilever that can support a heavy book for at least five minutes. What sort of supports will you use? How will you keep the structure stable? What can you use for weights? Keep track of your designs and find the prototype that best fits your needs.

Cantilever Bridge

IDEAS FOR SUPPLIES
2 cups of similar size • weighted objects • 2 popsicle sticks • several flat objects of similar weight

Cantilever bridges are beautiful. Have you ever traveled on one? While they have been part of engineering and architectural design since the 1800s, they are now slowly entering the bioengineering world. Let's go make some!

1 Place the cups and popsicle sticks far enough apart so that both sticks touch each other. The popsicle sticks should be on top of the cups and result in an overhang in only one direction. Place a few weighted objects on top of each popsicle stick for support.

2 Try to put one weight in the middle of the bridge. Can your cantilevers support the weight without having the bridge collapse? How much weight can it support? Do uneven amounts of weight on the cantilevers result in a stable bridge? Why or why not? Make a chart to record the amount of weight your cantilevers support.

3 Rearrange the cantilevers to support each other prior to supporting a weight in the middle. Make the popsicle sticks overlap each other. Do you think this will result in less or more weight required to support each cantilever? Why?

Chapter 6

HEALTHY LIVING

The fields of biological engineering and biomedical engineering arose from the need to develop better medical devices, instruments, and therapies to diagnose and treat different illnesses and injuries. Biomedical engineers work on making medical devices and instruments. Biological engineers use genetics to develop cures and therapies. Both fields are important to modern medicine and will continue to be necessary for developing new medical strategies in the future.

? **ESSENTIAL QUESTION**

How are biomedical and biological engineering used to make people healthier and their lives better?

Your Body, the Machine

biomechanics: the study of the movement of organisms.

Did you know that you probably performed all kinds of biomechanical feats while doing something as simple as sitting down to eat breakfast this morning? **Biomechanics** is the study of the movement of biological organisms based on certain laws of physics.

Through the use of biomechanics, athletes can learn to train better, injured people can recover the use of their limbs, and amputees can learn to use artificial limbs.

To understand biomechanics, you have to look at basic mechanics first. We learned in chapter 4 that force is needed to move an object. Remember how an airplane takes off? The forces of thrust and lift push the airplane into the sky, while the forces of drag and weight pull the airplane back to land.

Any kind of movement that you make uses force, too, and follows Newton's laws of motion. Flex your arm and bring your hand to your head. Can you feel how the muscle on top of your upper arm, called the biceps, is tight? Can you feel that the muscle on the bottom of your upper arm, called the triceps, is relaxed and stretched?

Now unflex your arm. What do your muscles do? What do they feel like? Your biceps loosens and stretches out, while your triceps gets tighter. The force is provided by your muscles! Your muscles work in pairs throughout your body to provide the force for your body to move. The triceps and biceps are an example of one working pair of muscles.

Together, the triceps, biceps, and bones in your arm make a working **lever**. Levers are **simple machines** that are used to move heavy things.

A lever consists of a **bar**, or rod, and a **pivot**, which is also called a fulcrum. The bar is what all the forces act on and balance on. A fulcrum serves as a point for the bar to move on. The heavy object that needs to be lifted is called the load.

The effort, or force, needed to move the load is provided by someone or something doing the work of lifting. You can arrange the bar, pivot, load, and effort in several ways.

Our body is full of different types of levers! There are first-class, second-class, and third-class levers in our body. You probably used at least a first-class and third-class lever when you ate your breakfast this morning.

Moving Muscles

Each of your muscles is made up of millions of muscle cells. Each muscle cell has many contracting units that contain the proteins actin and myosin. When your muscles contract, actin and myosin interact and cause each contracting unit in the muscle to get more compact. Your muscle cells all work at the same time to cause your entire muscle to contract and become more compact. When your muscles relax, actin and myosin also relax and don't interact. Each contracting unit goes back to a normal, relaxed state.

A first-class lever looks and works like a seesaw. The pivot is located in the center of the bar, with the effort and load on opposite sides of the bar. When you nod your head or look up and down, you are using this type of lever. Your head is the load, your neck muscles provide the effort, and the pivot is the bones in your neck. Try it out and feel the muscles in the back of your neck while you nod your head up and down.

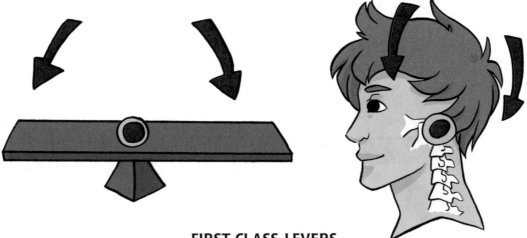

FIRST-CLASS LEVERS

A second-class lever is similar to a wheelbarrow. The pivot (the wheel) is located on one end, with the load in between the pivot and the effort. Standing on your toes is an example of this type of lever. Your body is the load, your calf muscles provide the effort, and your toe joints provide the pivot. Try this lever out and see if you can find the muscle in your calf that is providing the effort.

SECOND-CLASS LEVERS

A third-class lever has the pivot on one end and the load on the other end. The effort is applied in the middle of the pivot and the load. One example of the motion of a third-class lever in your body is you lifting a spoon to your mouth to eat. Your biceps provides the effort, the spoon is the load, and your elbow is the fulcrum.

THIRD-CLASS LEVERS

Understanding how levers work helps bioengineers design better prosthetics for people with missing limbs. A lever is only part of the equation for making a fully functional prosthetic. Microchips, brakes, and a hydraulic system are some of the other parts. Prosthetic limbs can be extremely complex to make, but are designed to work like the real limb.

Take a few steps and think about what is happening in your legs as you walk. Do you feel several muscles working? Do you feel that landing on your heel absorbs your weight? Can you feel how your knee bends and your lower leg swings forward to take a new step? Walking is a complicated process. Biomedical engineers are designing new technologies to create a smoother experience.

Artificial Organs

Do you remember the Tin Man in *The Wizard of Oz*, who wished he had a heart? Today, he might be able to get an artificial one that works like a real heart! Scientists have developed an artificial heart that can temporarily replace a damaged heart until the patient receives an **organ transplant**.

Replacing internal organs is much more difficult than replacing limbs. When an organ is replaced, the process is called an organ transplant. Usually, a damaged organ is replaced with a healthy organ from an organ donor. However, the right organ donor can be hard to find. People can spend many years on a waiting list, waiting for an organ that matches their needs to become available.

Did You Know?

Biomedical engineers at Duke University have grown human skeletal muscles in the lab. These muscles can contract just as muscles do in our bodies.

An artificial heart is a great solution for patients waiting for a real heart to become available.

With 3-D printing, scientists might be able to make functioning organs, such as hearts and kidneys. It would be very beneficial to be able to print 3-D organs from a patient's own cells. Right now, there is still considerable risk of the body rejecting an organ received during an organ transplant. The organ, such as a kidney, is not the patient's own, and the patient's **immune system** does not like it because it is seen as a **foreign** object that does not belong. A 3-D printed organ from the patient's own cells would eliminate this significant hurdle during transplant surgeries because the immune system would not view it as foreign.

Currently, a person can only live a few years with an artificial heart. Scientists hope that someday artificial hearts and other organs will be so well developed that people will be able to live out the rest of their lives without needing another transplant.

Smaller than Small

Nanotechnology is another field in which bioengineering is used to develop innovative medical procedures and products. Nanotechnology is the production of technology and materials at an extremely tiny level.

Just how small is nano? A nano is measured at 10^{-9} meters, or 1 billionth of a meter. Billions of **nanobots** could fit in a teaspoon. These are very tiny robots!

The idea of nanotechnology developed during the 1950s. An American physicist named Richard Feynman thought that scientific manipulation could occur at an atomic level, such as exchanging one atom from another. Today, nanotechnology is a lot more complex!

Nanotechnology has evolved to include **nanofibers**, nanobots, **nanofactories**, and nanomaterials. Though these are physically tiny objects, they have a big impact on the world around us! Mildred Dresselhaus is a scientist researching the properties of graphite and carbon, two common elements in our world. Her research has led to breakthroughs in nanotechnology that could one day replace traditional batteries.

Imagine driving a car powered by nanotechnology!

PS

A Boy and His Atom

Scientists at the company IBM have developed the ability to move single atoms. This is a terrific breakthrough in nanotechnology, and it also offers some different entertainment! Watch this movie made with atoms, which Guinness World Records has verified as the world's smallest stop-motion film.

boy and his atom 🔍

Nanotechnology can be useful in treating some diseases. Cancer is a disease that occurs when certain cells in the body change the way they grow, divide, and die. All living things are composed of cells. Humans are made up of many different kinds of cells, all of which have different functions.

Most cells have a **nucleus** that houses its DNA. Sometimes, an unwanted change occurs in the DNA, and the DNA **mutates**. The mutation might not have any affect on the cell or it may change the way the cell functions or grows. If the mutated DNA causes the cell to grow more rapidly than before, it could become a cancerous cell. Not all DNA mutations lead to cells becoming cancerous.

Did You Know?

The word *nanotechnology* comes from the Greek word *nanos*, which means "dwarf."

Cancer cells come from normal cells that have mutated some portion of their DNA.

The mutations might be different from one cancer patient to another, but the outcome is the same. The cancer cell can now grow out of control and make more of itself.

85

A group of cancer cells is called a **tumor**. It takes a lot of energy to replicate, so cancer cells need more energy and nutrients than a normal cell to survive. The cancer cell replicates so much that eventually it has to find another way to get more nutrients. One way it can do this is to find another area in the body to live.

The tumor can also make the body create new blood vessels to bring lots of nutrients right to it. That would be like you telling a restaurant to open up a drive through in your backyard so that you would never have to leave your house.

How do we get rid of these unwelcome cancer cells?

The immune system is one way to fight cancer cells. This system is normally hard at work removing bacteria and viruses, and sometimes it encounters and tries to kill cancer cells. It does this by constantly patrolling, keeping all parts of the body under surveillance. If something in our body does not belong there, including cancer cells, the immune system will try to get rid of it.

Did You Know?

About 86 percent of cases of skin cancer are caused by **ultraviolet (UV)** rays from the sun. The UV light rays have been shown to cause mutations in DNA. That doesn't mean you can't enjoy being in the sun, but wear sunscreen to block harmful sun rays!

Medicine is another way doctors fight cancer. One problem with medicine used to kill cancer cells is that it also destroys nearby non-cancerous cells. Another problem is that the cancer medicine gets distributed all over the body instead of heading directly toward the cancer.

Early Detection

When someone gets cancer, detecting it early and treating it correctly can be a matter of life and death. Early detection can be difficult in developing countries, where some people don't have access to medical care because it costs too much or it simply isn't there. Biomedical engineers such as Dr. Rebecca Richards-Kortum are helping to solve this problem. Her lab is developing cancer screening platforms that are low-cost and portable, allowing access to this life-saving technology all around the world.

Using nanotechnology, doctors might be able to better target these cancer cells. Cancer patients would be able to take lower doses of medicine with fewer side effects. Nanobots could deliver medicine to a specific target.

Another nano-device, called a **nanostar**, can help physicians and scientists find sneaky cancer cells. These atomic stars can find and enter cancer cells in the body. Once they enter a cancer cell, the nanostar lights up so a scientist knows that cell is cancerous.

Bioengineers are also researching ways to use viruses to fight cancer while not causing a person to become sick. A single virion has either DNA or RNA inside of it, depending on the virus. Scientists have modified the virion's DNA or RNA and coded it to find and enter cancer cells. The idea is that once the virus enters a cancer cell, it makes so many copies of itself that the cancer cell bursts and is destroyed. This type of therapy shows promise, but it is not perfected yet.

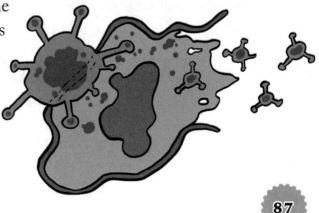

Bioengineering

Bioengineering can help improve the health of individuals, and it is also being used to advance global health, which is the health of entire populations. Improving global health uses all disciplines of bioengineering—biomedical engineering, biological engineering, and biomimetics.

Global health depends on a few basic things, including clean water, adequate food, clean energy, and affordable healthcare. Not everyone has access to these. When people lack these things, they are more likely to get sick. Why? Can you think of some other global health issues?

More low-cost solutions are needed to supply populations within developing countries with clean water, food, and healthcare. Many future bioengineering projects will need to focus on making simple, effective, low-cost devices and processes. This is not an easy task. Can you think of some ideas to improve global healthcare?

Bioengineering has provided some solutions for global health issues. Water purifiers are being developed that use nanotechnology. Several projects are underway to provide affordable, clean energy, including one using plants in solar panels.

? ESSENTIAL QUESTION

Now it's time to consider and discuss the Essential Question: How are biomedical and biological engineering used to make people healthier and their lives better?

Working Levers

Can you remember the examples of first-class, second-class, and third-class levers in your body? Let's find some more!

1 Picture a person doing pushups. What kind of lever are they using? Do a pushup to figure out what muscles you are mostly using. These muscles are providing the effort. What part of your body is the pivot? What is the load? Draw a picture in your engineering journal and label the parts of the lever.

2 Do you remember where a second-class lever is in your body? Find another one and draw it in your journal. Label the pivot, effort, and load. Use the same process and find a third-class lever in your body.

THINK MORE: Using the engineering design process, make one of the levers that exists in your body out of recycling materials. Design a prototype, test it, and redesign! Can you design a device that can lift and carry objects just as your arm does?

Brick Work

Lego has partnered with scientists to develop prosthetic devices with Lego creations as the missing arms. The prosthetic device supplies the motor and the child supplies the imagination to make their arm into anything they want it to be! You can see the Lego prosthetic arm in action. What would you design if you were to have a prosthetic arm?

Lego prosthetic Guardian 🔍

Lever Marble Run

IDEAS FOR SUPPLIES

multiple-sized popsicle sticks • cardboard or foam pieces • large binder clip (or cardboard made into a triangle) • marble or comparable item

Let's use levers to make a marble run. Don't forget to figure out which class of levers you use in your project!

1 Make several troughs out of cardboard or with smaller popsicle sticks glued to larger popsicle sticks. Make sure that the trough is large enough to accommodate a moving marble.

2 Feed one large popsicle stick or cardboard piece through the metal loop handles of the binder clip. Place another large popsicle stick or cardboard piece beneath the metal loop handles of the binder clip. Tape both popsicle sticks together at the ends—this provides a stable foundation for the binder clip and seesaw.

3 Make a seesaw by taping another trough to the clip portion. The seesaw should be able to move up and down.

4 Prepare a different part of the marble run by making another lever. Take one large trough and adhere it to a small popsicle stick with tape. The hinge should not be taped so tightly that the lever cannot open and close. Finally, create a stopping point for the marble by gluing a piece of cardboard at the end of the trough.

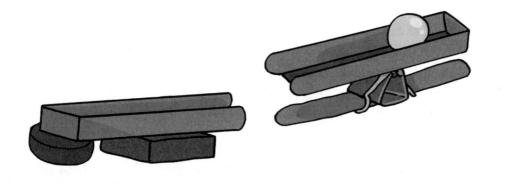

5 Design other ways to make the marble troughs move. Can you make places for the marble to get stuck? Can you find a way to make a marble stop and turn the other way? Can you make the marble drop from level to level?

6 Now it is time to try out your homemade marble run! What type of lever is the seesaw? What type of lever is the second component that the marble goes on?

THINK MORE: Make your marble run more complex! Add a spiral slide and a tunnel to the levers that you just made. Follow the engineering design method by first determining what you want to accomplish. Write and draw your plans in your engineering notebook and make a prototype. Remember, if your prototype does not function the way you intended, go back to the initial design and make changes.

Did You Know?

Engineering students at Swinburne University in Australia created the world's longest marble run in 2013. Their marble run was more than 4,221 feet long! You can see a video about their marble run at this website.

longest marble run 🔍

Nanobot Soccer Tournament

IDEAS FOR SUPPLIES

yogurt or coffee container lid • bead or kernel of rice
• magnets • corrugated paper • sandpaper

Researchers at the National Institute of Standards and Technology built a soccer stadium the size of a grain of rice and tiny nanobot soccer players. In this activity, you'll build a soccer stadium that is gigantic compared to the playing field that hosts the yearly nanobot soccer tournaments.

1 Clean off a yogurt or coffee container lid. Make two goals on the opposite sides of the lid with masking tape. Tear off a piece of masking tape, fold it slightly lengthwise in the middle, but do not tape the ends together. Place the sticky ends of the masking tape on the lid to make a ridge. Do this three times until you have made a goal. Complete the same process on the opposite side of the lid.

2 Tear off 1 inch of masking tape and fold over once. Continue to wrap the tape around itself until you have made a small rectangle, only slightly larger than a staple. Place a staple in the middle of the tape piece with a stapler. This is your soccer player. Prepare a second tape soccer player if playing with a friend. Use a bead or grain of rice as your soccer ball.

3 With magnets underneath the lid, guide your tape soccer players around the stadium. What happens if you use a piece of corrugated paper or sandpaper instead of the lid? Does the magnet move the player around as easily? Why or why not?

ACTIVITY

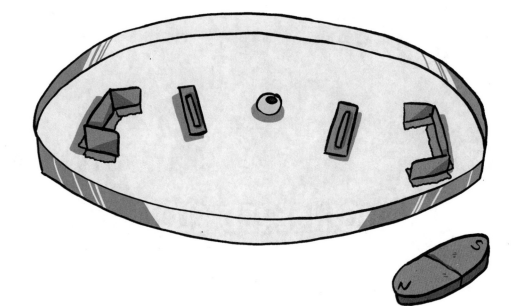

Did You Know?

Watch a nanobot soccer tournament.

NIST nanobot soccer 🔍

THINK MORE: Make a maze out of masking tape. Remember to set a goal and design a prototype first. Try to get your player from one side of the maze to the other. Scientists might use magnets to get nanobots containing medicine to the correct location in the body. What are some other ways to use magnets to improve the health and well-being of sick or injured people?

Chapter 7

BIOENGINEERED CLOTHING

Scientists believe that humans first began wearing clothing about 170,000 years ago. Our ancestors probably wore animal skins and fur. We have come a long way since then, but some of the best clothing still comes from animal, plant, and insect products. We still shear sheep for their wool to knit into sweaters and grow cotton to be picked and woven into shirts. These methods of making clothing are quite time-consuming, though, and scientists are using biomimetics to develop easier methods to make clothing.

Silky Insects

Beginning at least 7,000 years ago, silk was used to make clothes in China. For many years, the process of making silk was a heavily guarded secret. We now know that silk is made by silkworms and other insects. A silkworm is born the size of a pinhead and is fed mulberry leaves until it reaches 10,000 times its original weight.

bone plate: a thin sheet
of bone that is often used
in facial or bone fracture
surgeries.
scaffold: a framework.
resorb: to dissolve and
break down.

bone plate: a thin sheet of bone that is often used in facial or bone fracture surgeries.

scaffold: a framework.

resorb: to dissolve and break down.

WORDS TO KNOW

? ESSENTIAL QUESTION

What kind of clothing products have been developed using biomimicry?

At a certain time, the silkworm begins to spin silk and make a cocoon around itself. Silkworms have silk glands that produce a jelly-like substance made from digested mulberry leaves. This substance hardens when it is exposed to air.

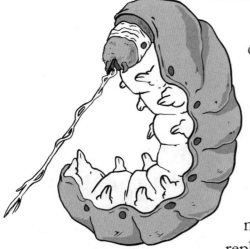

A silkworm makes its cocoon out of one continuous thread. About eight or nine days after the silkworm's cocoon is finished, the silk can be harvested.

Silk is also made by spiders. Spider silk is comparable to steel in strength, and it is also much lighter. The combined quality of strength and lightness of spider silk has many scientists thinking of new ways to replace steel with silk.

For example, scientists have been experimenting with making screws and **bone plates** out of spider silk. These would replace the metal screws and plates that are often needed during surgeries to fix complex bone fractures. They would also be useful for surgeries needed to fix facial injuries. These screws seem to provide a **scaffold** onto which bone can grow. The hope is that once the bone has reformed, the silk would be **resorbed** and disappear!

Did You Know?

You can see silkworms in action!

PS

Science channel silkworms 🔍

cellulose: the plant fiber in wood pulp.

defense mechanism: a method of protecting oneself from a predator.

synthetic: not found in nature.

WORDS TO KNOW

Spider silk is considered so strong that scientists are also looking at making bulletproof vests from it.

Making silk is a very expensive process. Many innovative people have tried to invent alternatives to silk. In 1855, Georges Audemars was the first to use liquid mulberry bark pulp and rubber to make a fabric that had the same qualities as silk. In the 1920s, rayon, another silk-like fabric, was introduced. Rayon is made from the **cellulose** in wood pulp or bamboo.

One company is using bacteria to make cellulose fabric sheets that can be placed on a mannequin and shaped into a shirt! Another company is making yarn out of leftover animal parts. Scientists continue to make artificial silk, but nature still makes the best silk!

Printed Pants

You probably have a printer at home from which you can print out assignments that you need for school. Could you print out a 3-dimensional (3-D) object, such as a toy? If you are like most people, probably not! However, 3-D printers are becoming more and more common.

Did You Know?

Scientists and engineers are hoping that 3-D printing is going to solve many different problems. Take a look at this video to see what 3-D printing is about.

PBS 3-D printing 🔍

Slimy Clothes?

Recently, scientists have begun to investigate using hagfish slime to make a silk-like thread. The hagfish can make a liter of slime in a second. It uses the slime as a **defense mechanism** against any predator that tries to bite it. When a predator tries to attack a hagfish, it comes away with a mouthful of slime and the hagfish gets away unscathed. You can see hagfish slime here.

Scientific American hagfish 🔍

Using a computer program that enables 3-D design, people can design anything, such as toys, tools, household objects, and clothing. This 3-D design is then sent to a printer that is able to print out your object, layer by layer, in plastic, rubber, or other materials.

Although humans have been wearing animal furs and skins for a long time, today many people don't want to wear such products. Some people would prefer a **synthetic** leather that is not made from animal skins. Currently, technology is being fine-tuned to allow the 3-D printing of leather and skin. Eventually, clothes and shoes might be made from 3-D printed leather instead of animal skins!

Some companies are developing ways to 3-D print food. Would you consider eating food that was 3-D printed?

From Burrs to Velcro

While nature might make wonderful materials to wear, some products used in clothing have been developed by people who simply observe nature.

Do you have any Velcro on your body right now? Shoes, cold-weather clothing, sleeping bags, and tents often use Velcro fasteners. In 1941, a Swiss engineer named George de Mestral and his dog were taking a hike in the Alps. At one point, he discovered that his clothes and his dog had become covered in burdock burrs. Most people might be annoyed by these clinging burrs, but de Mestral was intrigued. He used a microscope to take a closer look and discovered tiny hooks on the burr that were able to catch onto microscopic loops present on clothing and his dog's fur.

After making several prototypes, de Mestral made Velcro with two components. One piece had little loops and another piece had nylon hooks. Today, Velcro is used all around the world as a fastener on clothing or shoes. It is even used by astronauts in space to keep objects, such as their dinner plates, from floating away in zero gravity!

The word *Velcro* comes from the words *velvet* and *crochet*, which is a French word for "hook."

Piney Clothes

Pine cone fabric is another example of an idea that came from observing nature. Female pine cones open and close according to the amount of humidity in the air.

If you go outside after a storm, it will be hard to find a pine cone on the ground that has its scales open. Rain and humid conditions cause the pine cone to close its scales. Dry conditions cause female pine cones to open.

Pine cones can open and close because their scales have two layers that go in opposite directions. The outer layer of the scale responds to water by swelling so much that it causes the pine cone scales to close. When it is dry out, the same outer layer shrinks and pulls the pine cone scales open.

Why do you think female pine cones do this?

Did You Know?

Humans eat a part of pine cones—pine nuts! These are used in sauces and salads.

Bioengineers have created fabric that is breathable. It allows the user to cool down if they have been exercising. In this fabric, two layers with stiff fibers run opposite one another. When a person sweats, the fabric absorbs the sweat and flaps in the fabric open to allow cool air to flow through. When the fabric is dry, the flaps close. Although this is the opposite of what a pine cone does in nature, the mechanism is similar. What else in nature might be a good source of inspiration for making fabric?

Nature has developed some amazing adaptations during millions of years that are just waiting to be studied. While all biomimetic prototypes might not yield a useful product, it is fun to just observe and learn from nature.

? ESSENTIAL QUESTION

Now it's time to consider and discuss the Essential Question:
What kind of clothing products have been developed using biomimicry?

Test Tensile Strength

IDEAS FOR SUPPLIES

*cardboard box • duct tape • metal clips with or without hook
• paper clips • squares of aluminum foil, paper, and tissue,
all the same size • plastic bag • small weights • scale*

**Tensile strength is a material's ability to withstand breaking. We
are going to perform a test that looks at the tensile strength
of different materials. A tissue has different strength than a
sheet of aluminum, which is good because they are used in
different ways. Would you like to blow your nose with a sheet
of aluminum or wrap a sandwich in a tissue? Let's look at
the tensile strength of different materials in your house.**

1 Fold all the flaps of the box inward except for one. Cut half of the
unfolded flap off lengthwise. Stabilize the flap by adding strips of duct
tape to each side along that cut edge. Stabilize a resealable bag by
adding strips of duct tape along the opening edge on both sides.

2 If you don't have metal clips with hooks, unwind a paper clip and
wrap it around the metal clip,
leaving the end as a hook.

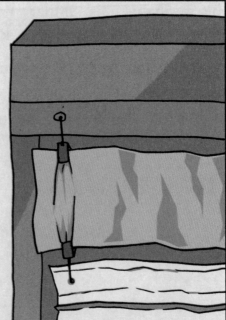

3 With a pencil, make two
holes in the flap of the box and
in the top of the resealable bag.
Place two metal clip hooks into
the holes in the flap and two
metal clip hooks into the holes
of the bag. You are now ready
to try an experiment!

ACTIVITY

4 Collect samples of different materials (aluminum foil, a tissue, paper, plastic wrap) and make sure they are all the same size and approximate thickness. If your metal clips have teeth, use masking tape on any item where you place a metal clip.

5 Attach one material to all four clips. Make sure that the resealable bag is not touching the ground. What can you use to slowly add weight to the resealable bag? How much weight can you add before the material rips?

6 When the material has ripped, remove the weights and measure them on a scale. In your engineering notebook, record the material and the amount of weight needed to rip the item. Since you used equivalent sizes of material, you can compare their strength. The more weight the material can support without breaking, the stronger the material.

THINK MORE: Can you make a **hybrid** material consisting of two materials that you tested, stronger than either of those two materials alone? Remember that to evaluate how strong it is, you need to make sure that the hybrid material is the same weight as both components separately.

WORDS TO KNOW

hybrid: something that is composed of two different things.

101

Pondering Pine Cones

IDEAS FOR SUPPLIES

2 pine cones • sealable plastic bags • paper towel soaked in water

Have you ever observed pine cones in trees or after they have fallen on the ground? In this activity, you'll see what pine cones do in dry and wet environments.

1 Put one pine cone in a sealable plastic bag by itself and the other in a bag with a paper towel that has been soaked in water. Seal both bags.

2 Leave the bags for 15 minutes. Do you observe any changes after 15 minutes? Write down your observations in your engineering journal.

3 After one hour, look at your pine cones again. What is different about them? Why? Why do you think the pine cones react this way to moisture? Record your observations and hypothesis in your science journal.

THINK MORE: Why do you think female pine cones open and close while male pine cones tend to stay closed? What purpose does opening serve for the female pine cones?

Did You Know?

Some species of pine trees can live for thousands of years. Bristlecone pines are considered to be the longest living trees and have been found to survive for thousands of years.

Chapter 8

FARMING

Traditional farming has always required a tremendous amount of effort. Planting, harvesting, and caring for the soil and **livestock** all require lots of energy. More and more, **agricultural** and bioengineering methods are being combined to **streamline** the production, harvest, and distribution of food on traditional farms.

Food for Thought

A farmer can only stay in business if enough crops are sold to produce a **profit**. There are many obstacles to contend with before a piece of fruit or a vegetable makes its way to the produce section of a store near you. One issue is the timing of when the produce will ripen and when customers will want to eat it.

Bioengineering

? ESSENTIAL QUESTION

How can bioengineering change the way we produce food?

Today, most of us see tomatoes in the produce section all year round, but that was not always the case. Just 150 years ago, people were able to eat only whatever was grown locally. If you lived in the northern United States, there were no tomatoes available in the winter. Modern transportation and biological engineering are two reasons someone in Vermont can enjoy tomatoes in January.

Canning is one way that bioengineering has intersected with agriculture to make farms more efficient. About 200 years ago, the process of canning food arose as a method to preserve food.

Canning involves exposing food to a high heat and preserving it precisely in a tin can or a glass jar. The heat kills off any bacteria that could render the food toxic for humans. Adding vinegar and other acidic components makes the environment inside the jar unsuitable for most bacterial growth.

Today, canning is done in factories under specific conditions to largely remove the risk of contamination. However, there is still risk of contamination during canning.

Did You Know?

The French military issued a reward for a method to preserve food, and in 1810, a French candy maker named Nicolas Appert received the prize for his method of canning.

You Can, Too!

Before canning became something that was done on a large scale in factories, people did their own canning at home, and they still do! You can find instructions on canning at this website. Have an adult help you and follow all the guidelines so that your canned food is safe to eat!

USDA home canning 🔍

The bacterium *Clostridium botulinum* causes an illness called **botulism** that can often be fatal. This bacterium lives in the soil and loves to grow where there is no oxygen present. If it manages to survive the heating process during canning, it is more than happy to grow in the low-oxygen environment found inside a jar! If you ever open a jar or can of fruits or vegetables and find a horrible smell, chances are good that bacteria are lurking inside, so just throw it away!

Genetic Engineering

Besides canning fruit and vegetables, there are other methods for making produce available year round. One of these methods is the use of **genetic engineering**. It involves changing the DNA of the crop, including adding, altering, or removing genes.

Genetic engineering requires technology that only became available in the last 40 years.

Bioengineering

Before this, people had been **selectively breeding** plants to have certain characteristics. Breeding is different than using the technology available today, but the outcome from both can occasionally yield similar results.

Gregor Mendel, the Austrian monk considered to be the "Father of Genetics," bred pea plants. He observed that the parent plants gave certain characteristics to their offspring. Mendel discovered that there were hereditary units, later defined as genes, that determined how tall a pea plant would be or what color flowers it would have.

Imagine a farmer having two types of pea plants. One plant yields tasty, sweet peas, but only a few of them. The other plant yields peas that taste like cardboard, but it makes a lot of them. What would happen if the farmer could combine the best of those characteristics? They might get an offspring that would yield lots of tasty peas!

Today, it is possible to make changes to a plant's DNA through biological engineering. For example, some tomatoes have been altered so that their ripening gene is removed. These genetically altered tomatoes can no longer ripen. They stay green until they are sprayed with the ripening gas, **ethylene**, so that they can ripen at a certain time.

Have you ever grown tomatoes? It takes a while for the plant to grow, to flower, and to bear little green tomatoes. All of a sudden, the tomato ripens and soon turns slightly mushy. What happens when farmers try to ship ripe, mushy tomatoes across the country?

Because of genetic engineering, tomatoes can now be shipped when they are green. Then they can be ripened with ethylene just before they are placed in the produce aisle at the supermarket.

Currently, there is a debate about genetically altered food. Some food has been raised to be resistant to pesticides, which means more pesticides can be used on weeds while not hurting the crop. But the pesticide can still hurt the environment, including insects and animals.

Did You Know?

Many different terms are used to describe the genetic manipulation of plants, including "recombinant DNA biotechnology," "genetic engineering," and "biological engineering."

Food From Animals

Farm animals can also be genetically altered. As of 2015, the USDA has only approved the sale of genetically altered farm-raised salmon to consumers.

Labels

According to the U.S. Department of Agriculture (USDA), most corn, cotton, and soybeans used by consumers since 2012 are genetically engineered versions of the food. The European Union requires all genetically modified food to be labeled as such. The USDA does not require this labeling. Do you think food should be labeled as genetically engineered? Why or why not?

Bioengineering

WORDS TO KNOW

Hello, Dolly!

On July 5, 1996, Dolly the sheep, the first **cloned** mammal in the world, was born in Scotland. Dolly was an exact genetic copy of another six-year-old sheep. Scientists had been able to clone other organisms, such as plants, frogs, and bacteria, for years, but many people worried that cloning a sheep would lead to cloning humans. The process is extremely difficult and scientists need to learn much more before this can happen. However, many farm animals that display superior quality are being cloned. What do you think of cloning?

Some genetically altered animals are used to produce medicine for certain illnesses. For example, a genetically altered goat has been made that produces a certain medicine in its milk. This allows the medicine to be made in larger quantities than was possible before. The process does not seem to hurt the goat.

Did You Know?

Some farm-raised salmon have been genetically altered to grow faster. That means the fish will be full-grown and ready to eat in a shorter period of time than wild-caught salmon.

The United States is not the only country to make genetically altered animals. Scientists in other countries are working to make a genetically altered chicken that does not get sick with an avian flu virus. What do you think about the practice of genetically altering animals?

One problem we face today is that the world's population is growing by leaps and bounds and it is difficult to feed everyone. Genetically altered food might be a solution to this problem, if it does not harm humans when consumed during a long period of time.

? ESSENTIAL QUESTION

Now it's time to consider and discuss the Essential Question:
How can bioengineering change the way we produce food?

Be a Biological Engineer

IDEAS FOR SUPPLIES

2 small ripe strawberries • sealable plastic bag • water • liquid soap •
salt • paper towels • 2 glasses • sieve • cold 90-percent ethanol

Genetics, the study of DNA and inheritance, plays an important role in biological engineering. Scientists often extract DNA from cells and perform experiments with it. You can extract DNA from strawberries!

Caution: Do not eat or drink your solution.

1 Wash the strawberries, remove the tops, and place in a sealable bag. Squish the strawberries as much as possible in the bag with your hands. Put 2 teaspoons of tap water into the bag and squish some more.

2 Put 4 drops of soap into the water-strawberry mixture. Mix by squishing and try to not get too many bubbles forming in the bag. Add a pinch of salt to the mixture and give it another quick mix.

3 Put a paper towel inside a sieve. Place the sieve on top of a clean glass and pour the contents of the bag through the sieve. Let the liquid collect in the glass. Pour the liquid into a tube or a very small clean glass. Have a parent help you pour 5 teaspoons of ice-cold ethanol into the tube or glass. Gently swirl the contents of the glass for several minutes. You should be soon able to see a stringy glob. That is strawberry DNA!

TRY MORE: Try to isolate your own DNA. Spit out 2 teaspoons worth of saliva into a glass. Skip adding the water. Put in the same amount of soap, salt, and ethanol as you did for the strawberry experiment. Gently swirl the contents of the glass. What do you see?

Aquaponics

IDEAS FOR SUPPLIES

tomato seeds • soil • pots • betta fish • 1-gallon plastic or glass container • water filter • water conditioner • betta fish food pellets • water conditioner • Styrofoam piece or plastic lid from container

Aquaponics is a system of growing plants and fish together so that each benefits from the existence of the other. In this project, you'll set up a system in which a fish relies on plants, which rely on the fish!

1 Plant your tomato seeds in a pot filled with soil.

2 Purchase a betta fish, food pellets, water filter, and water conditioner from your local pet store. Ask an adult for help in preparing the bowl using the instructions included with the water conditioner. Allow all the water to reach room temperature before adding some dechlorinated water to the gallon container that will house the betta fish. Adding cold fresh water will cause your fish to go into shock!

3 Prepare a piece of Styrofoam or the lid of a yogurt cup by making a small pencil-sized hole in the center of it and two additional holes on each side. Attach string to each hole on each side and tape the strings securely to the sides of the aquarium.

4 When your tomato plants are 2 inches high, gently pull one from the pot, shake the soil from the roots, put it in the center hole of the lid or Styrofoam and place in your mini-aquarium. Don't worry about the dirt particles that will fall to bottom of the tank.

5 Gently pull a second plant and place it in a new pot of soil and water it. Place both your potted tomato plant and the mini-aquarium in an area inside your house that receives sunlight. Draw a picture of your plants on the first day in your engineering notebook.

ACTIVITY

6 Maintain your fish by feeding it the recommended amount of food each day and cleaning its aquarium weekly.

7 Watch your plant and fish grow! Why are we growing a plant in a fish tank? Which plant is growing the fastest, the one in the soil or the one in the fish tank? Record your observations in your engineering notebook.

THINK MORE: What does the plant supply the fish with? What does the fish supply the plant with? Can you think of other ways to grow plants without using soil? Why might this type of agriculture be beneficial as the world's population grows?

A Bit About the Betta Fish

Betta fish live in rice paddy fields in a minimal amount of water, such as a footprint-sized water puddle. They are also called Siamese fighting fish and usually need to live alone because they are aggressive toward their own species and other types of fish. They have a labyrinth organ, which allows them to go up to the surface of the water and take a breath through their mouth. They can also breathe through their gills.

If you take care of your fish, it usually will live for two to three years, sometimes even as long as eight years! Caring for your fish means feeding your fish every day and changing the water every week.

Vertical Farming

IDEAS FOR SUPPLIES
*succulent plant • soil • zip ties • 6 water bottles • hole punch •
phillips screwdriver • large popsicle sticks or small wood slats*

Since space is often limited in an urban area, people will often have rooftop gardens. They have also begun to do vertical growing. In this project, you'll grow your own vertical garden.

1 With an adult's permission, purchase a succulent plant. The Graptopetalum succulent is easy and quick to grow and **propagate.** If you purchase a small plant, grow it for a few months and then gently pull off the larger leaves on the bottom of the plant with a gentle side-to-side motion until you hear a snap. Put each of the removed leaves on a plate and leave them in a warm area for several weeks to grow roots. There is no need to put them in soil or water them. Most of the leaves will turn into individual plants!

2 To make a pyramid structure, cut off the bottom third of six water bottles. Trim some more of each bottle off and cut two tabs 180 degrees from each other, as shown in the illustration. In three of the bottles, puncture one hole in the very bottom underneath each tab. Punch a hole into each tab.

3 Prepare a triangle frame out of popsicle sticks and glue and set aside. Pour dirt into the three bottle bottoms without holes. Place a succulent into each. Secure two tabs of different bottle bottoms together with a zip tie. Secure the third bottle bottom with another zip tie. Secure each outer bottle bottom to a side of the triangle frame.

ACTIVITY

WORDS TO KNOW

propagate: to grow, to increase the amount of something.

4 Continue to make the next layer of plants in the same manner, making sure you use the bottle bottoms that have holes on the bottom. Secure each layer to the frame. You can also glue each bottle bottom to the ones beneath it for a more stable structure. Prepare the top layer in the same manner. Stabilize your structure further, if you need to.

5 Put your baby succulents in each of the bottle bottoms. If you water the top succulent, water will trickle down to the bottom plants. Succulents do not like to be watered often. Wait until the soil is dry to water your plants.

THINK MORE:

How are your plants growing? Are they growing evenly? Do you think this a feasible way to grow crops? Why or why not?

Did You Know?

Singapore's Jack Ng grows bok choy and cabbages indoors in his A Gro-Go "farmscraper." Using trays stacked in aluminum towers reaching 30 feet high, Ng says his farmscraper grows more than five times the vegetables produced in traditional farming. He grows plants close to grocery stores so his vertical farm cuts down on transportation costs and reduces pollution.

acceleration: the change in speed or direction of an object.

acid: a substance that loses hydrogen in water. Examples include lemon juice and vinegar.

acidic: from acids, which are chemical compounds that taste sour, bitter, or tart.

adapt: to change in response to something.

adhesive: a substance used to stick materials together.

aerodynamic: having a shape that reduces the amount of drag when the object moves through the air.

agriculture: the practice of farming plants and animals.

amber: fossilized tree resin used in early static electricity experiments.

amplitude: the height of a wave.

anemometer: a device that measures wind speed and pressure.

armature: the spinning part of a motor, made of tightly coiled wires.

atom: the smallest particle of matter that cannot be broken down by chemical means. An atom is made up of a nucleus of protons and neutrons, surrounded by a cloud of electrons.

bacteria: tiny living microbes that live in animals, plants, soil, and water. Bacteria are decomposers that help decay food. Some bacteria are harmful and others are helpful.

bar: used in a lever to balance the weight of an object and the force applied to move that object.

base: substance that accepts hydrogen from another substance. Examples include baking soda and ammonia.

basic: from bases, which are chemical compounds that often feel slippery in water and taste bitter.

BCE: put after a date, BCE stands for Before Common Era and counts down to zero. CE stands for Common Era and counts up from zero. These nonreligious terms correspond to BC and AD. This book was printed in 2016 CE.

biodegradable: capable of being broken down in nature.

bioengineering: the use of engineering principles applied to biological function to build devices, tools, or machines for a human need.

biology: the study of living things.

biomechanics: the study of the movement of organisms.

biomimetics: the study of nature for the purpose of creating products or processes based on something in nature.

blueprint: a design for a building.

bone plate: a thin sheet of bone that is often used in facial or bone fracture surgeries.

botulism: an often fatal sickness caused by a bacterium called *Clostridium botulinum*.

calcium: a mineral found in shells and bones.

cancer cell: a normal cell that changes to grow out of control.

canning: the process of safely preserving food in a jar or can.

cantilever: an extension of a building or bridge that appears to be unsupported, but is supported at one end.

cellulose: the plant fiber in wood pulp.

climate change: changes to the average weather patterns in an area during a long period of time.

clone: to make an organism that is genetically identical to another organism.

cochlea: the organ that translates sound into information that nerve cells can send to the brain.

complement: to complete or enhance by providing something additional.

component: a part of something.

decalcification: the process of losing calcium.

decibel: a unit for measuring loudness.

defense mechanism: a method of protecting oneself from a predator.

discharge: the removal of electrons from an object.

DNA: deoxyribonucleic acid. The substance found in your cells that carries your genetic information, the "blueprint" of who you are.

drag: the force that opposes motion due to friction.

ear canal: a tube that allows sound waves to reach the ear drum.

ear drum: a membrane of the middle ear that vibrates in response to sound waves. Also called the tympanic membrane.

echolocation: the use of active sonar to locate an object by bouncing sound off the object.

electric charge: when there is an imbalance of electrons, either too many or not enough, and the electrons flow to fix the imbalance.

electricity: a form of energy caused by the movement of tiny particles called electrons. It provides power for lights, appliances, video games, and many other electric devices.

electrolyte solution: a liquid or paste in a battery that allows for the flow of electric current.

electron: a part of an atom that has a negative charge. It can move from one atom to another.

element: a substance whose atoms are all the same. Examples of elements include gold, oxygen, and carbon.

engineer: someone who uses science, math, and creativity to design products or processes to meet human needs or solve problems.

ethylene: the hormone that causes ripening in plants.

exoskeleton: a skeleton on the outside of a body.

force: a push or pull applied to an object.

foreign: from outside the body or country.

foundation: the base of a home or other building that is partly underground. The foundation supports the weight of the building.

frequency: the number of sound waves that pass a specific point each second.

friction: the rubbing of one object against another. Also the force that resists motion between two objects in contact.

gearbox: a unit within a machine with interlocking toothed wheels.

generator: a machine that converts mechanical energy into electricity.

genes: inherited material that has the instructions to make an organism with certain traits and characteristics.

genetic engineering: to change the DNA of an organism.

gland: an organ that makes and releases substances the body needs.

glider: a large flying construct that can be flown like a kite or navigated by a person.

gravity: a force that pushes down on objects and also pulls things together in space.

greenhouse gases: a gas such as water vapor, carbon dioxide, and methane that traps heat in the atmosphere and contributes to warming temperatures.

hertz: a unit for measuring pitch.

hybrid: something that is composed of two different things.

hydroelectric: generating electricity from the energy of flowing water.

hydrophobic: when a substance stays separate from water.

imaging: producing an image by means other than visible light.

immune system: the network of cells in your body that fights illnesses.

implant: an object that is placed into something, such as a human body.

instantaneous: immediate.

ion: an atom with a positive or negative electrical charge. This means it is missing an electron or has an extra electron.

landfill: a huge area of land where trash gets buried.

larynx: the organ that produces sound in the human body, also known as a voice box.

lattice: strips of material that are crossed and fastened together with diamond-shaped spaces in between.

lever: a device that can move something.

lift: the force that lifts the plane once it reaches a certain speed due to a difference in air pressure on the wings.

livestock: animals raised for food and other products.

load: the weight of something.

load-bearing: supporting the weight of a structure.

loudness: how soft or loud a sound is.

magnetic field: the invisible area around a magnet that pulls objects to it or pushes them away.

mass: how much matter is in an object.

matter: anything that takes up space and has mass.

medium: any gas, liquid, or solid material containing matter.

membrane: a bendable, sheet-like lining.

microbe: an organism that is so small it can be seen only with a microscope.

molecule: a very small particle made of combinations of atoms.

motion: the action or process of moving or changing place or position.

mutate: to change.

nanobot: a microscopic robot.

nanofactory: a manufacturing system used at the atomic level.

nanofiber: atomic-level strands of material.

nanostar: an atomic star.

nanotechnology: the use of tools and materials at the atomic level.

nerve cells: the parts of the nervous system that conduct information to and from the brain.

neutron: a tiny particle inside the center of an atom that carries no charge.

nucleus: the compartment within a cell that houses DNA. Plural is nuclei.

organic architecture: the use of the surrounding environment as part of the design of a building.

organism: any living thing, such as a plant or animal.

organ transplant: a surgery in which a defective organ such as a kidney or lung gets replaced by a new organ.

ornithopter: an aircraft that must flap its wings to fly.

papillae: small, rounded bumps on a part or organ of the body. Singular is papilla.

particle: a tiny piece of matter.

photoacoustic: the use of light and sound to make an image from within the body.

photon: a particle of energy in sunlight.

photosynthesis: the process through which plants create food, using light as a source of energy.

physicist: a scientist who studies physics.

physics: the science of how matter and energy work together. Matter is what an object is made of. Energy is the ability to perform work.

pitch: how high or low a sound is, depending on its frequency.

pivot: a hinge.

pollinate: to transfer pollen from the male part of a flower to the female part so that the flower can make seeds.

profit: the money made in a business after all the expenses have been paid.

propagate: to grow, to increase the amount of something.

proton: a tiny particle inside the center of an atom that carries a positive charge.

prototype: a model of something that allows engineers to test their idea.

renewable energy: a form of energy that doesn't get used up, including the energy of the sun and the wind.

resorb: to dissolve and break down.

rotor: the rotating part of a generator.

scaffold: a framework.

selective breeding: taking two plants with different characteristics to make an offspring with certain desirable characteristics.

silicon: an element used in solar panels that can interact with photons to release electrons.

simple machine: a tool that uses one movement to complete work.

solar panel: a device used to capture sunlight and convert it to usable energy.

sonar: an acronym for **SO**und **N**avigation **A**nd **R**anging, in which sound is used to detect objects.

sound wave: the invisible vibrations in the air that you hear as sound.

species: a group of living things that are closely related and can produce young.

static electricity: the buildup of an electric charge on the surface of an object.

streamline: to make a process simpler and more effective.

synthetic: not found in nature.

thrust: the force that propels an object forward.

toxic: something that is poisonous or harmful.

tumor: a group of cancer cells.

turbine: a machine with blades turned by the force of water, air, or steam that changes one type of energy into another.

ultrasonic: sound with a pitch too high for humans to hear.

ultrasound: the use of sound to make an image of something inside a body.

ultraviolet (UV): invisible light radiated from the sun.

vibration: a quick back-and-forth movement.

virus: a non-living microbe that can cause disease.

weight: the result of gravity acting on the mass of an object.

Metric Conversions

Use this chart to find the metric equivalents to the English measurements in this book. If you need to know a half measurement, divide by two. If you need to know twice the measurement, multiply by two. How do you find a quarter measurement? How do you find three times the measurement?

English	Metric
1 inch	2.5 centimeters
1 foot	30.5 centimeters
1 yard	0.9 meter
1 mile	1.6 kilometers
1 pound	0.5 kilogram
1 teaspoon	5 milliliters
1 tablespoon	15 milliliters
1 cup	237 milliliters

RESOURCES

BOOKS

Bioengineer. Gray, Susan H. Cherry Lake Publishing. North Mankato. 2014.

Careers in Biotechnology. Hall, Linley Erin. Rosen Publishing. New York. 2012.

DNA Detective. Kyi, Tanya Lloyd. Annick Press. Toronto, Canada. 2015.

Bioengineering in the Real World. Marquardt, Meg. ABDO. Minneapolis. 2016.

TRY A GAME!

Copernicus Strain: The Bioengineering Game

WEBSITES

Biomimetics: Design by Nature at National Geographic:
ngm.nationalgeographic.com/2008/04/biomimetics/tom-mueller-text

Biomimicry Institute: biomimicry.org

National Aeronautics and Space Administration (NASA):
grc.nasa.gov/www/k-12/UEET/StudentSite/dynamicsofflight.html#forces

National Nanotechnology Initiative: nano.gov/node/240

U.S. Department of Energy: energy.gov/eere/education/teach-and-learn

ESSENTIAL QUESTIONS

Introduction: What product do you use in your own house
that was created through bioengineering?

Chapter 1: What are the different ways that sound is used in bioengineering?

Chapter 2: How does bioengineering help us get the electrical energy we need?

Chapter 3: What products do you use in your home that were inspired by nature?

Chapter 4: If you were designing a car, where in nature would you look for ideas?

Chapter 5: If you were designing a house inspired by
nature, what elements would you include?

Chapter 6: How are biomedical and biological engineering
used to make people healthier and their lives better?

Chapter 7: What kind of clothing products have been developed using biomimicry?

Chapter 8: How can bioengineering change the way we produce food?

RESOURCES

QR CODE GLOSSARY

Page 6: *airandspace.si.edu/exhibitions/codex/codex.cfm#page-1*

Page 13: *scientificamerican.com/video/what-does-the-universe-sound-like-2013-09-13*

Page 18: *animalplanet.com/tv-shows/animal-planet-presents/videos/ the-ultimate-guide-to-dolphins-secrets-of-dolphin-sonar*

Page 23: *youtube.com/watch?v=JHKUvxmN-wk*

Page 29: *archive.org/stream/experimentsobser00fran#page/n7/mode/2up*

Page 33: *apps2.eere.energy.gov/wind/windexchange/schools/projects.asp*

Page 39: *treehugger.com/clean-technology/fish-inspired- wind-farms-are-10x-more-powerful.html*

Page 45: *oceanacidification.noaa.gov/AreasofFocus/OceanAcidificationMonitoring.aspx*

Page 53: *science360.gov/obj/video/642db496-d506-432e- 85b4-4e38f75d9142/newtons-three-laws-motion*

Page 58: *history.com/topics/inventions/wright-brothers/ videos/wright-brothers-test-flight-1909*

Page 59: *howthingsfly.si.edu/activities/forces-flight*

Page 60: *youtube.com/watch?v=n_q_DD_4LNg*

Page 69: *pbslearningmedia.org/resource/phy03.sci.phys. mfw.bbcantilever/firth-of-forth-cantilever-bridge*

Page 74: *fractalfoundation.org/videos*

Page 85: *research.ibm.com/articles/madewithatoms.shtml#fbid=oaP9utUjrOF*

Page 89: *theguardian.com/artanddesign/architecture-design-blog/2015/ jul/22/lego-prosthetic-arm-that-kids-can-hack-themselves*

Page 91: *youtube.com/watch?v=-lX2sYCh7ME&feature=youtu.be*

Page 93: *nist.gov/public_affairs/factsheet/nanosoccer.cfm*

Page 95: *sciencechannel.com/tv-shows/how-do-they-do-it/ videos/how-do-they-do-it-silk-from-worm-spit*

Page 96: *pbs.org/video/2339671486*

Page 97: *blogs.scientificamerican.com/cocktail-party-physics/the-hagfish-goes-high-fashion*

Page 105: *ucfoodsafety.ucdavis.edu/files/26457.pdf*